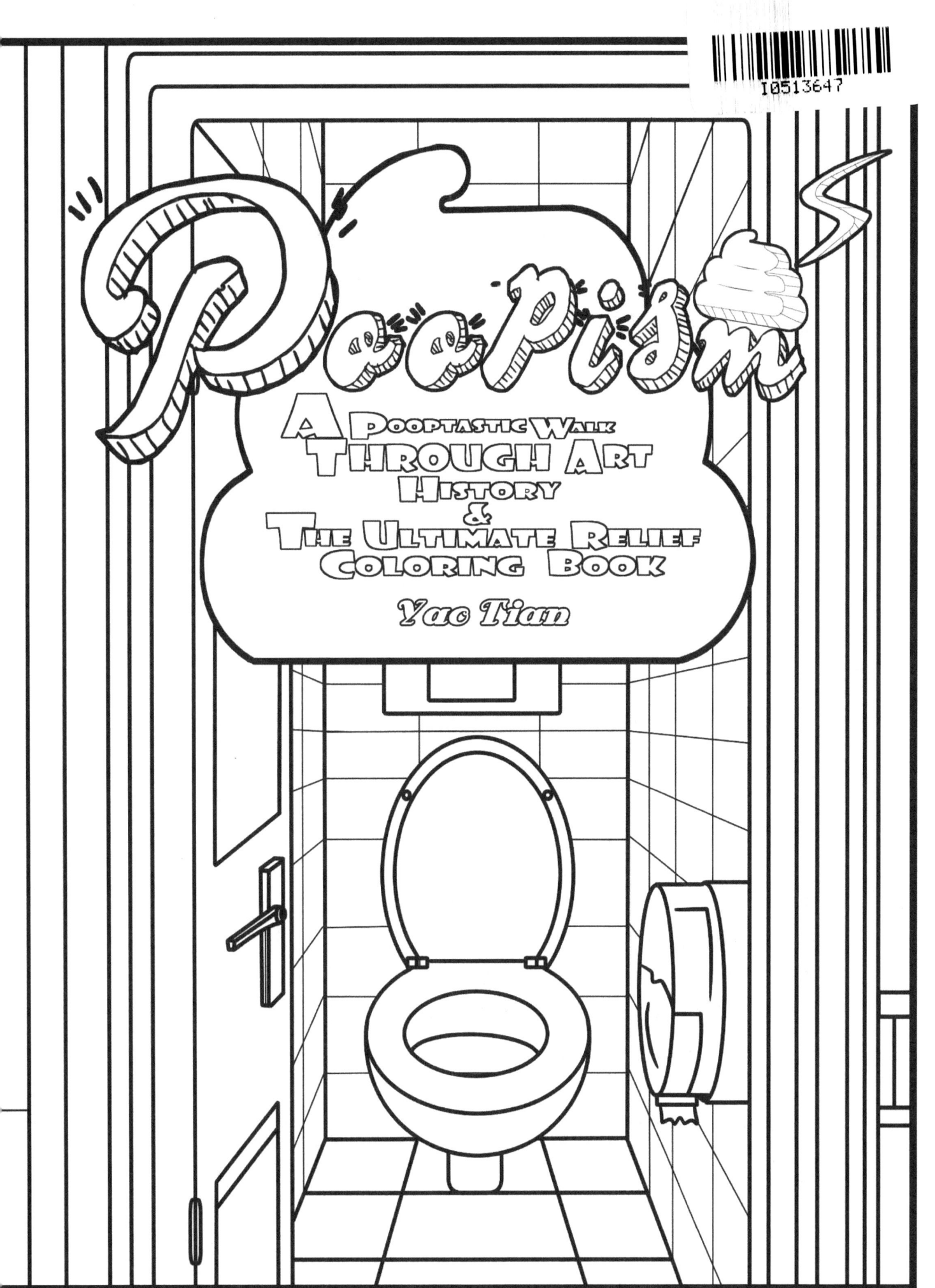

This book poopifies 30 masterpieces from art history. How many of the original artwork can you recognize?

Copyright © 2018 Yao Tian

All right reserved. No part of this book may be reproduced or transmitted in any form or by any means, electronic or mechanical, including photocopy, recording or any information storage and retrieval system, without permission in writing from the author.

Design: KwokYeow Tan, Ye Tian

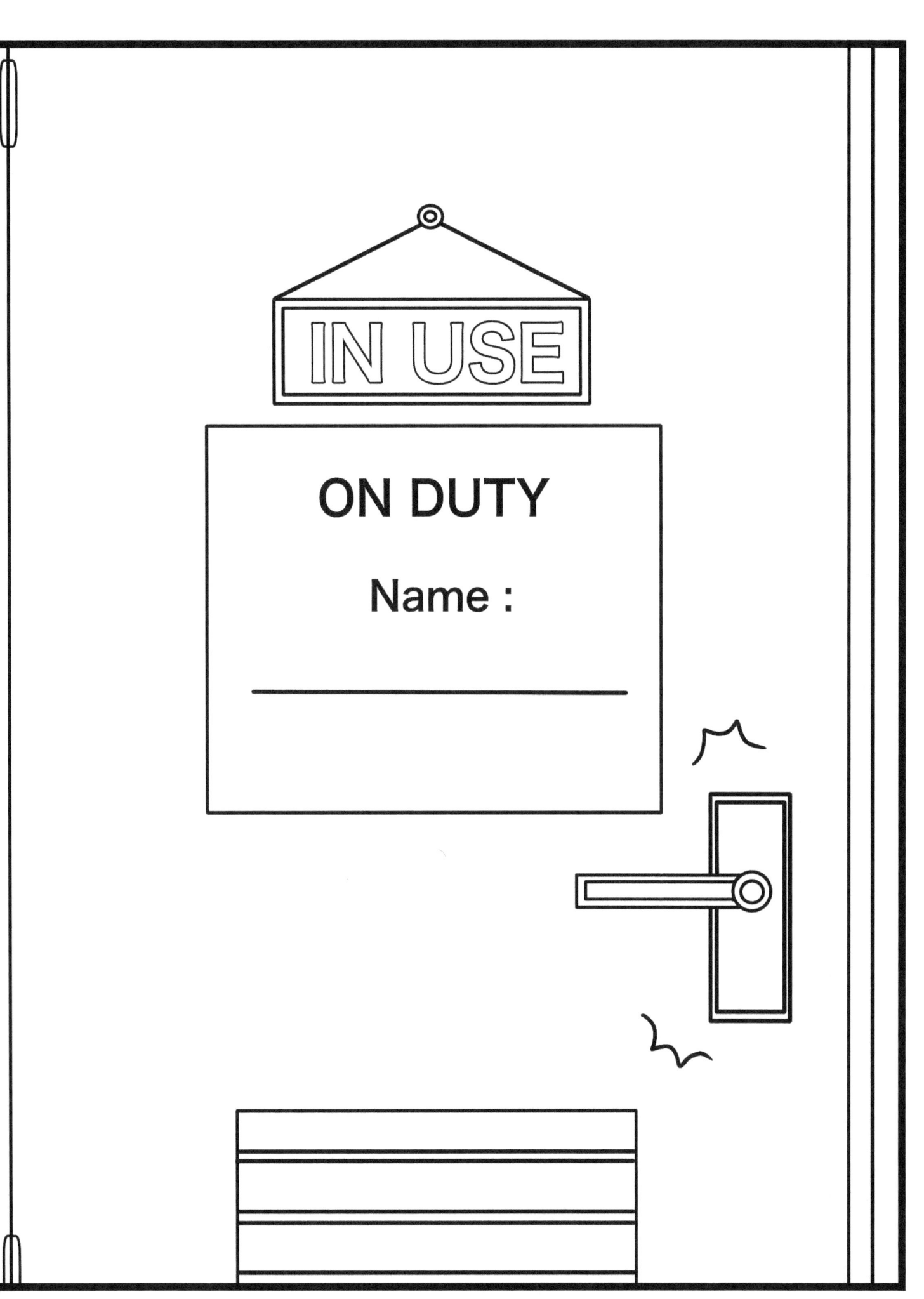

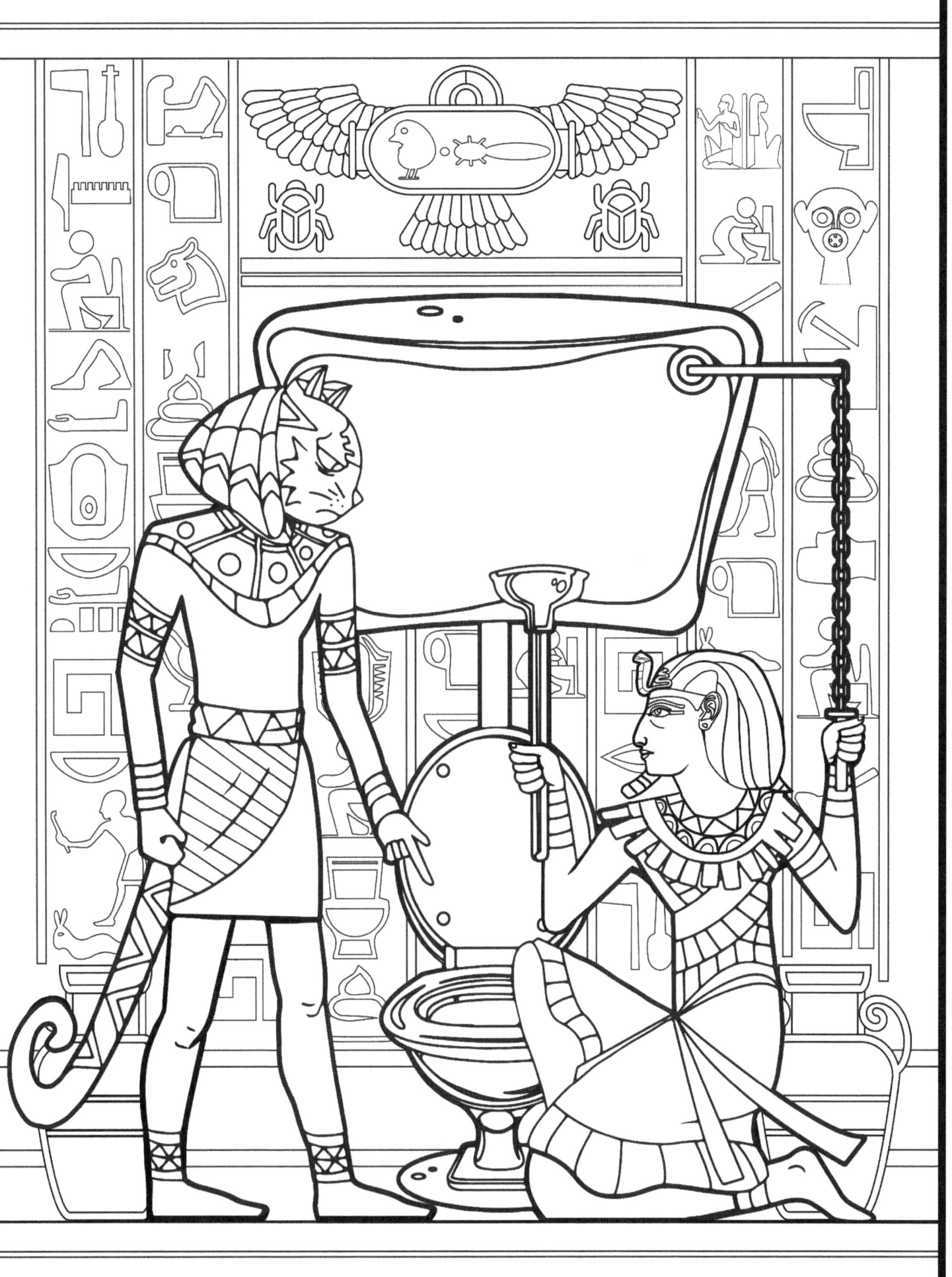

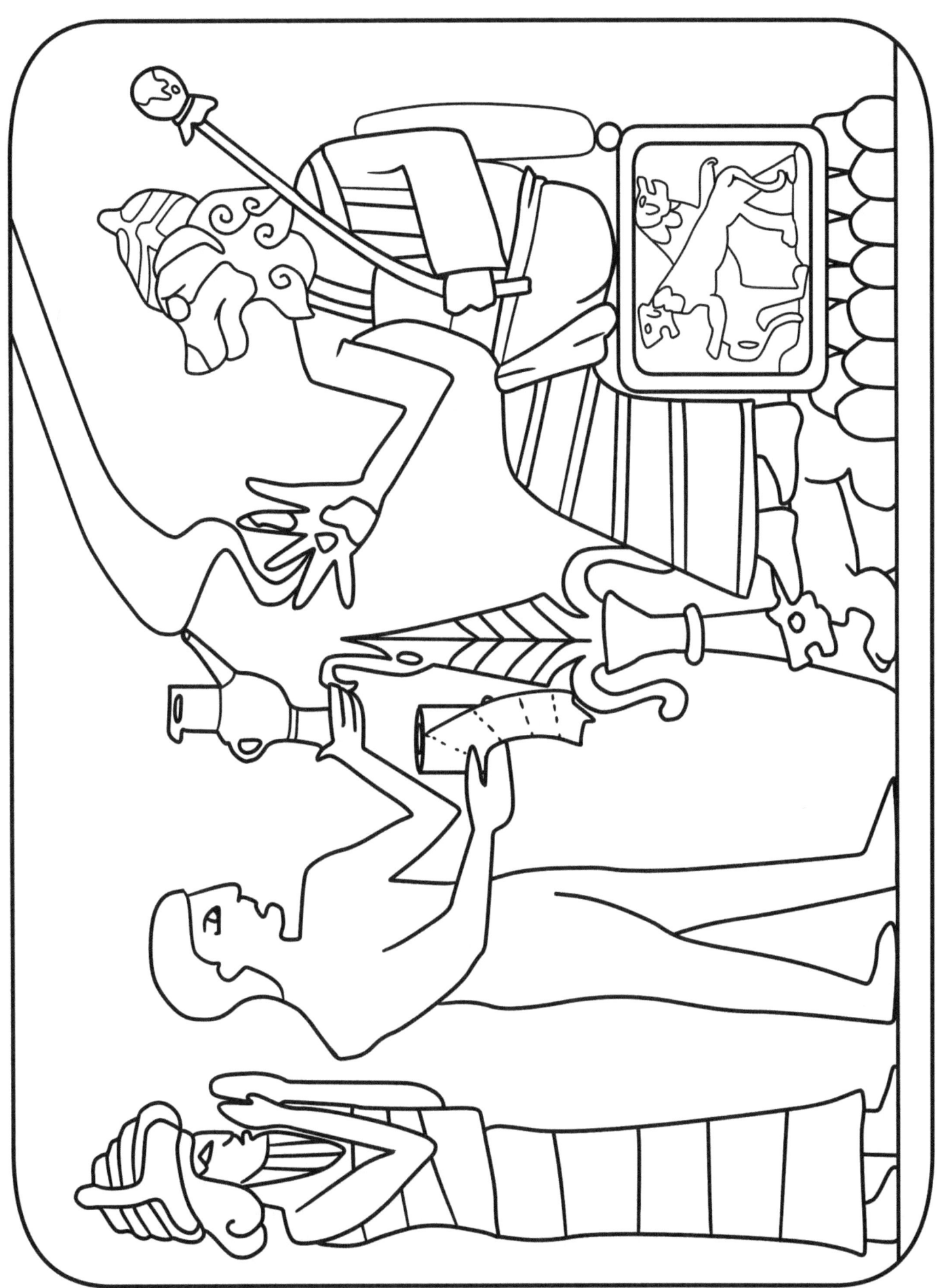

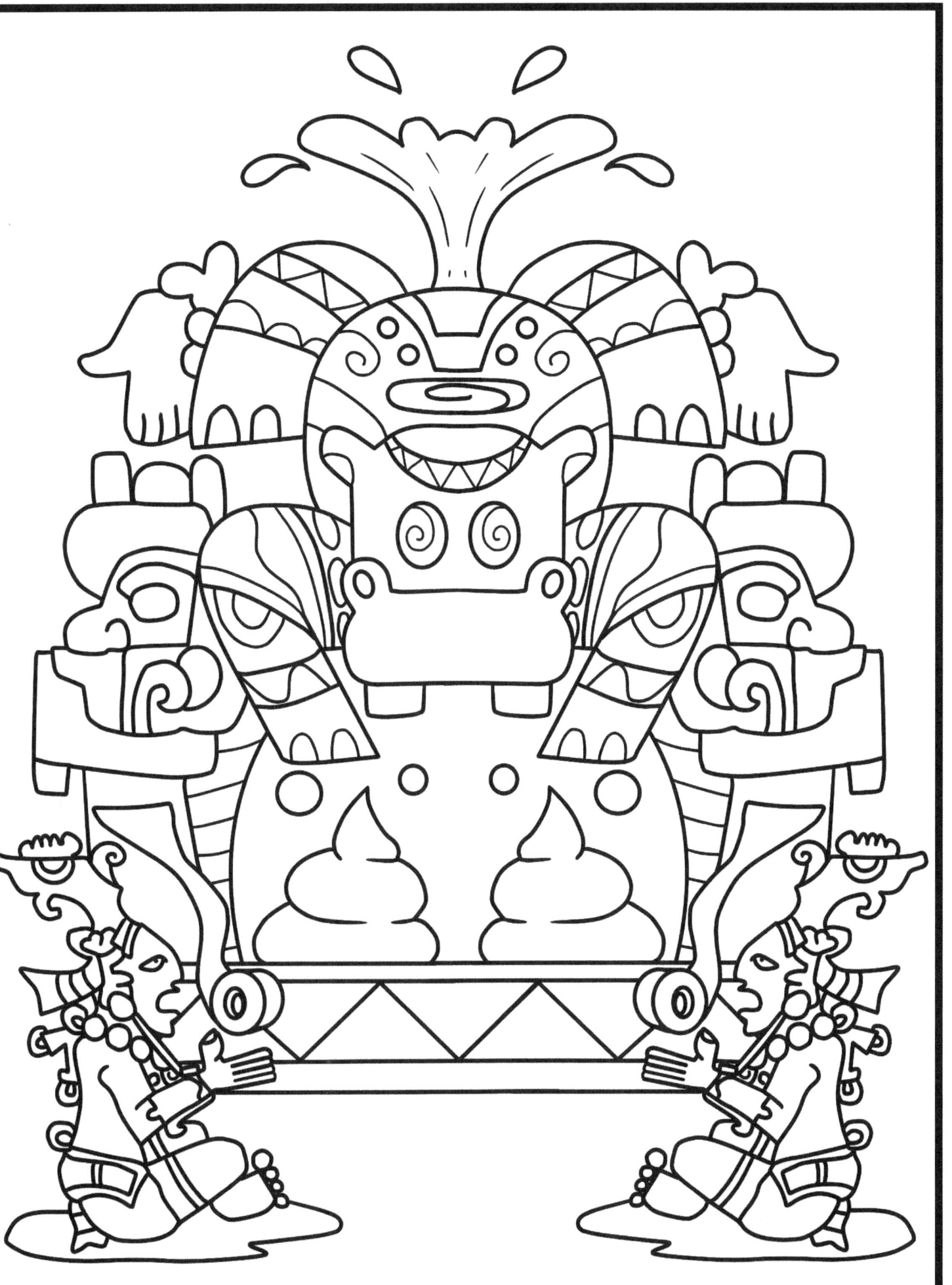

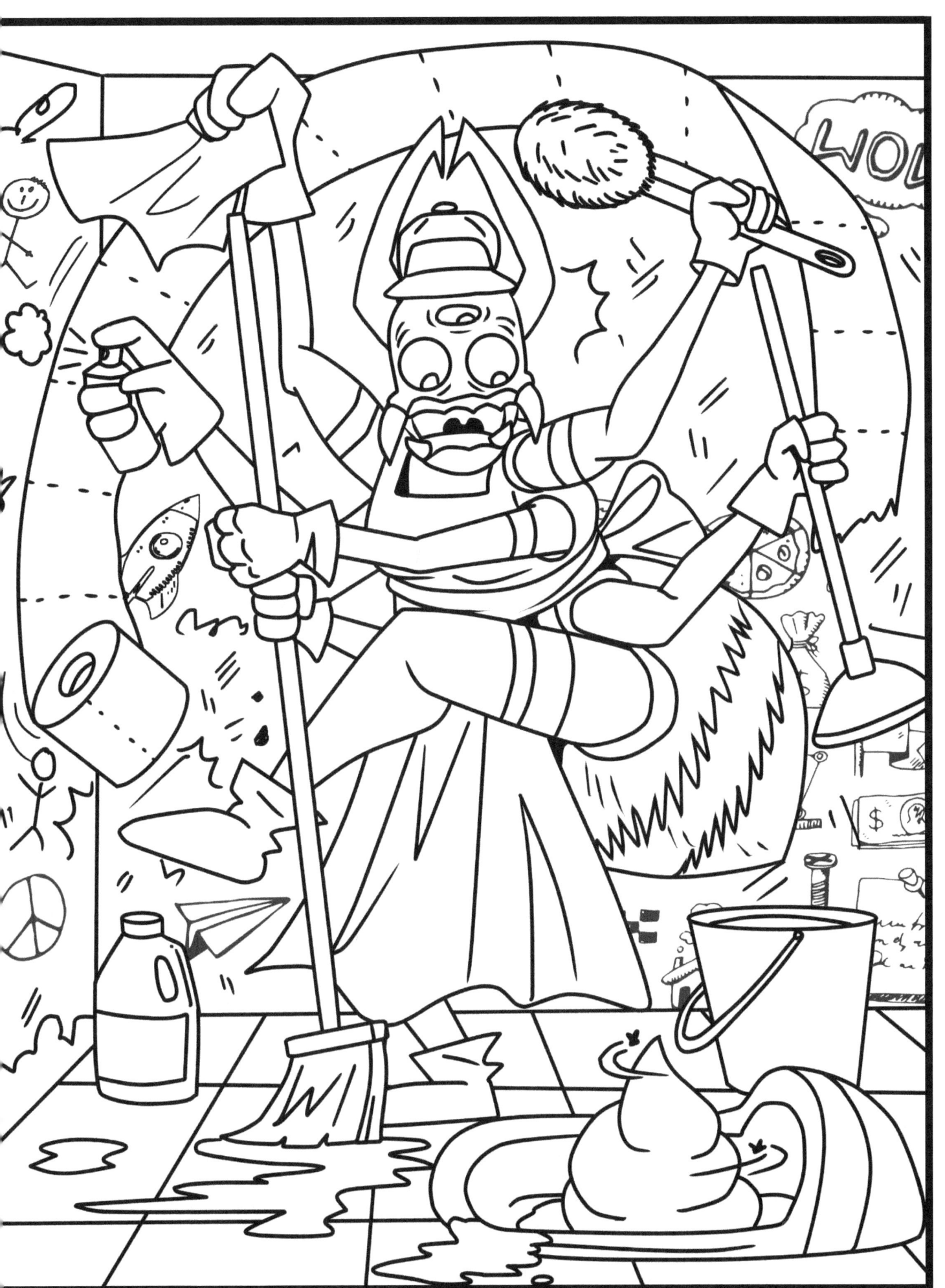

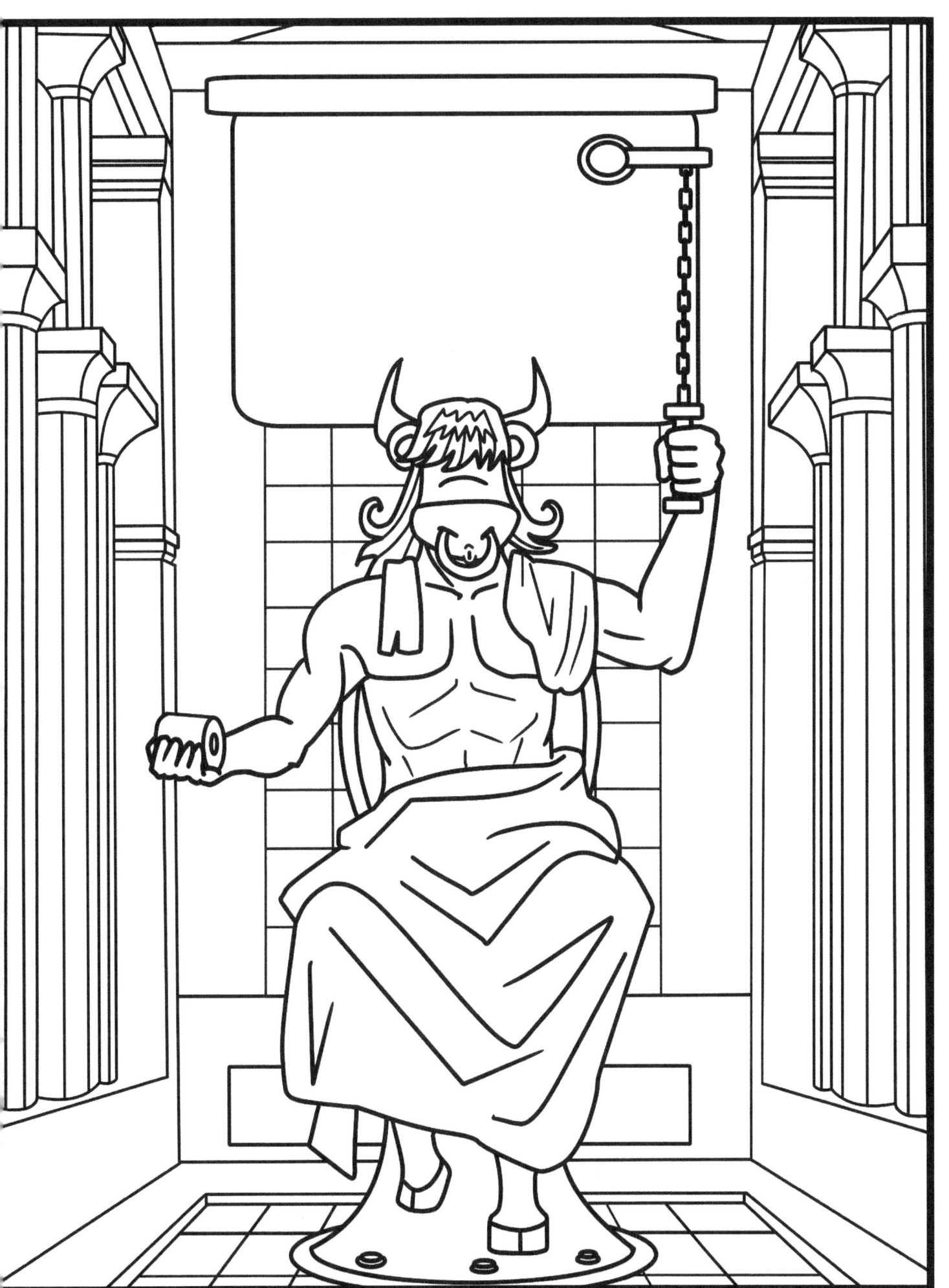

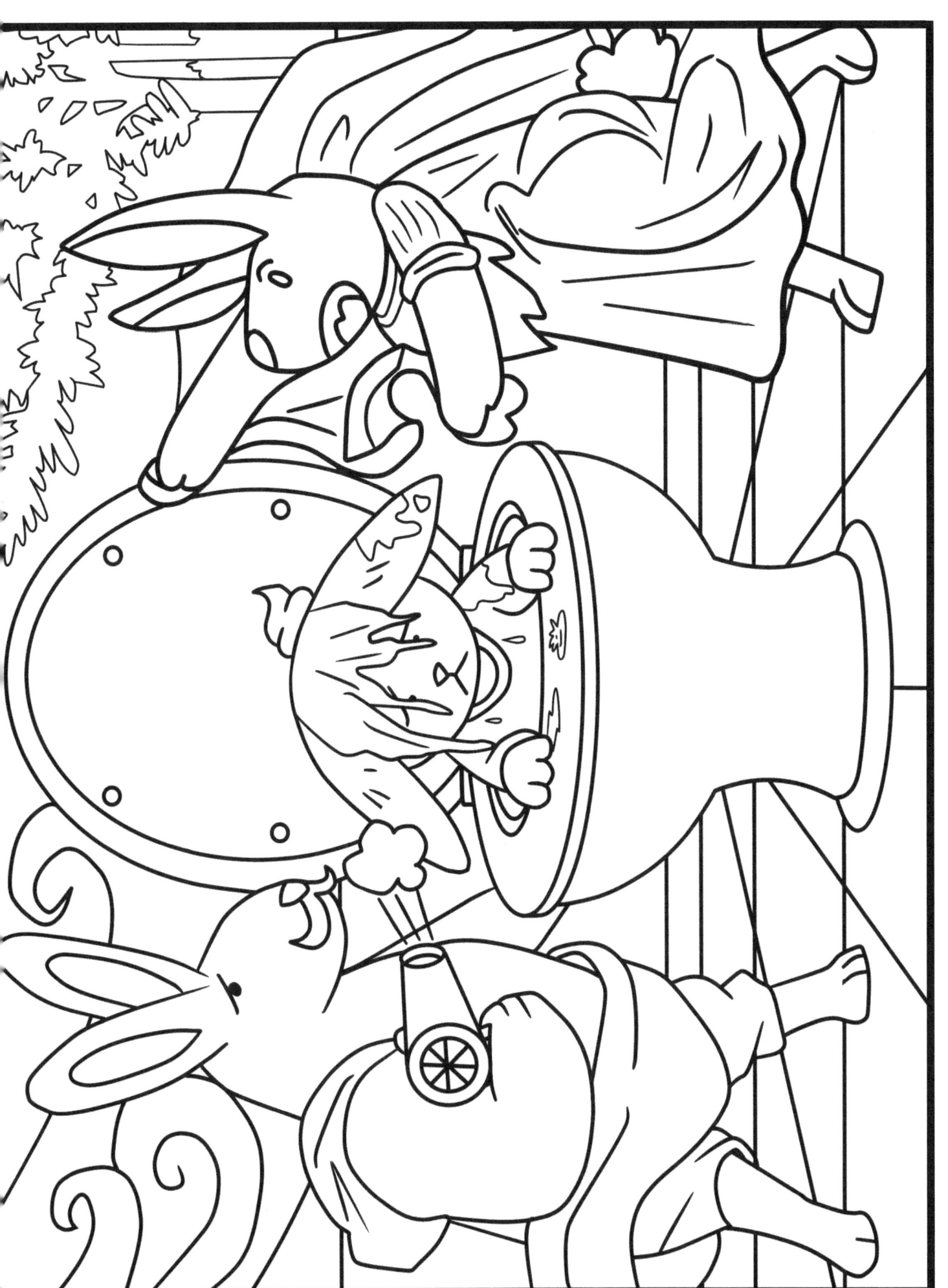

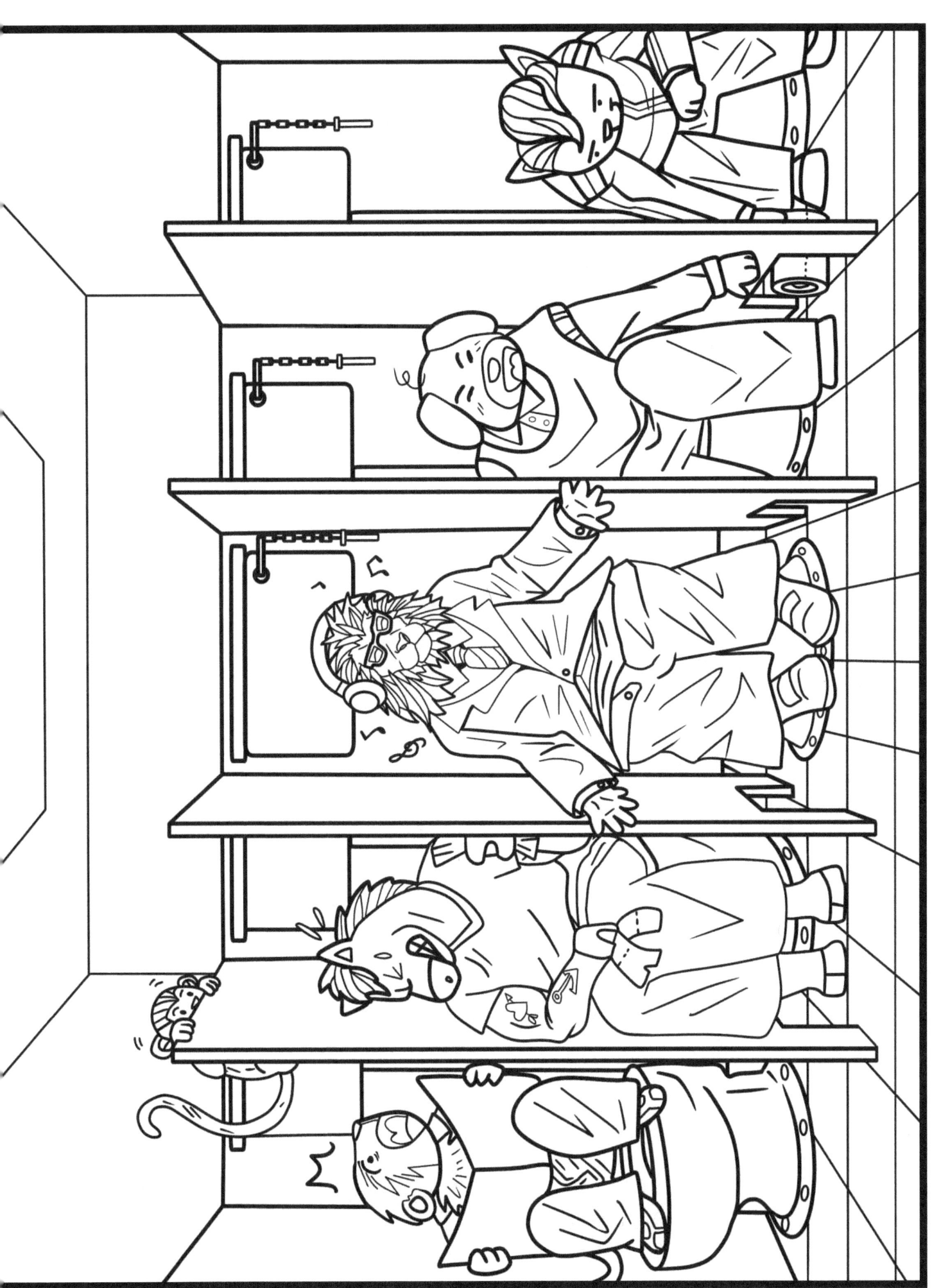

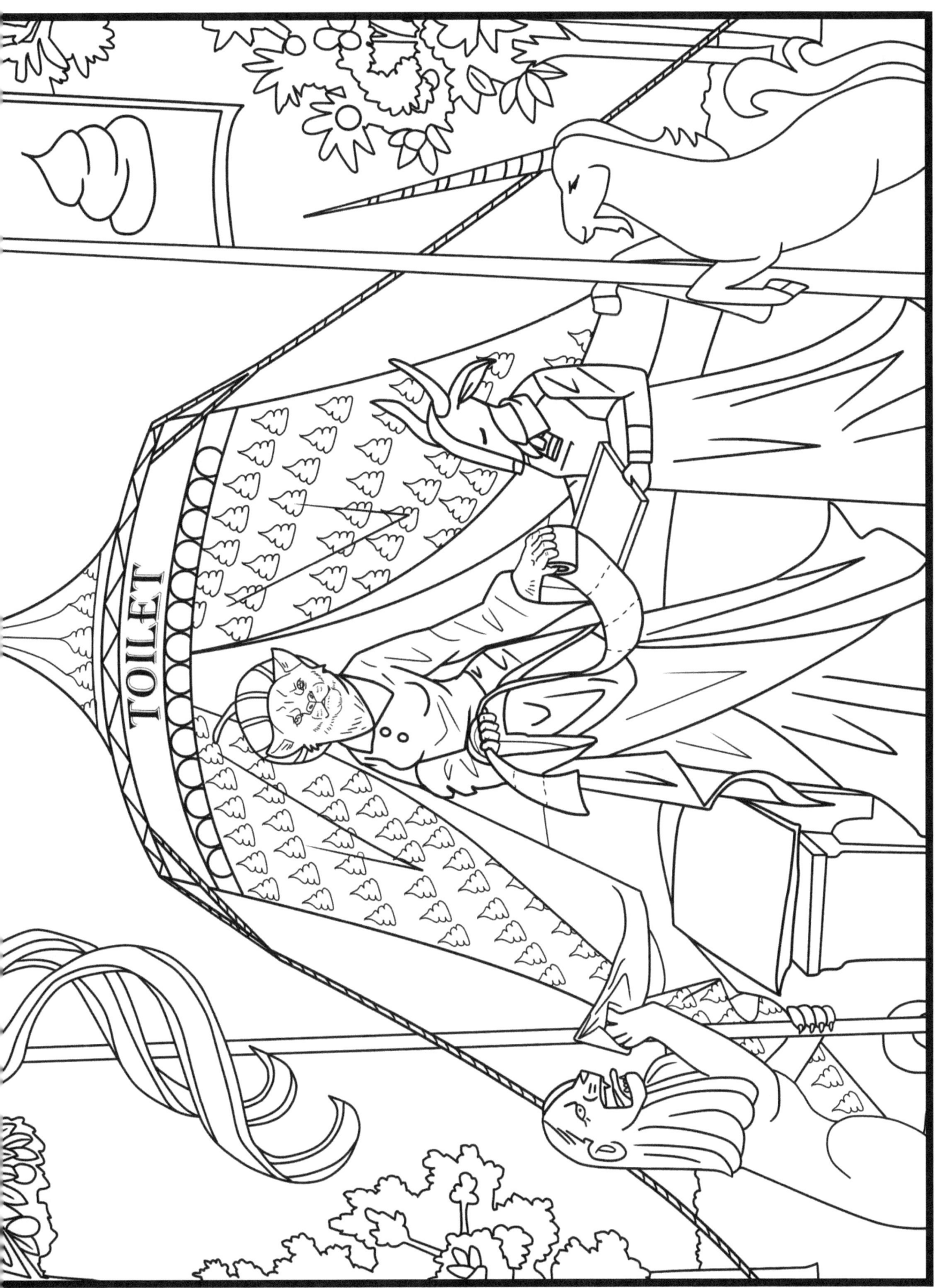

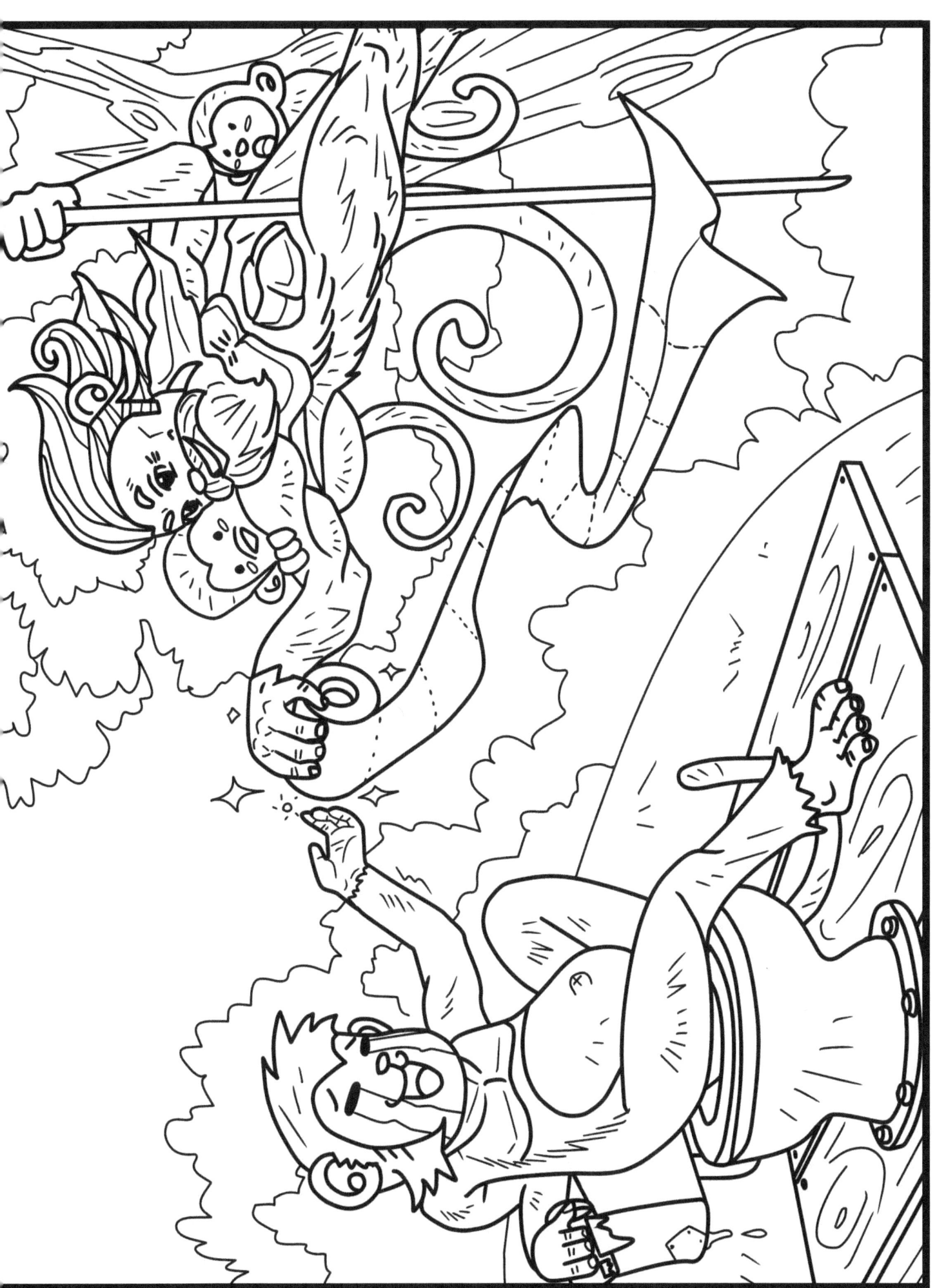

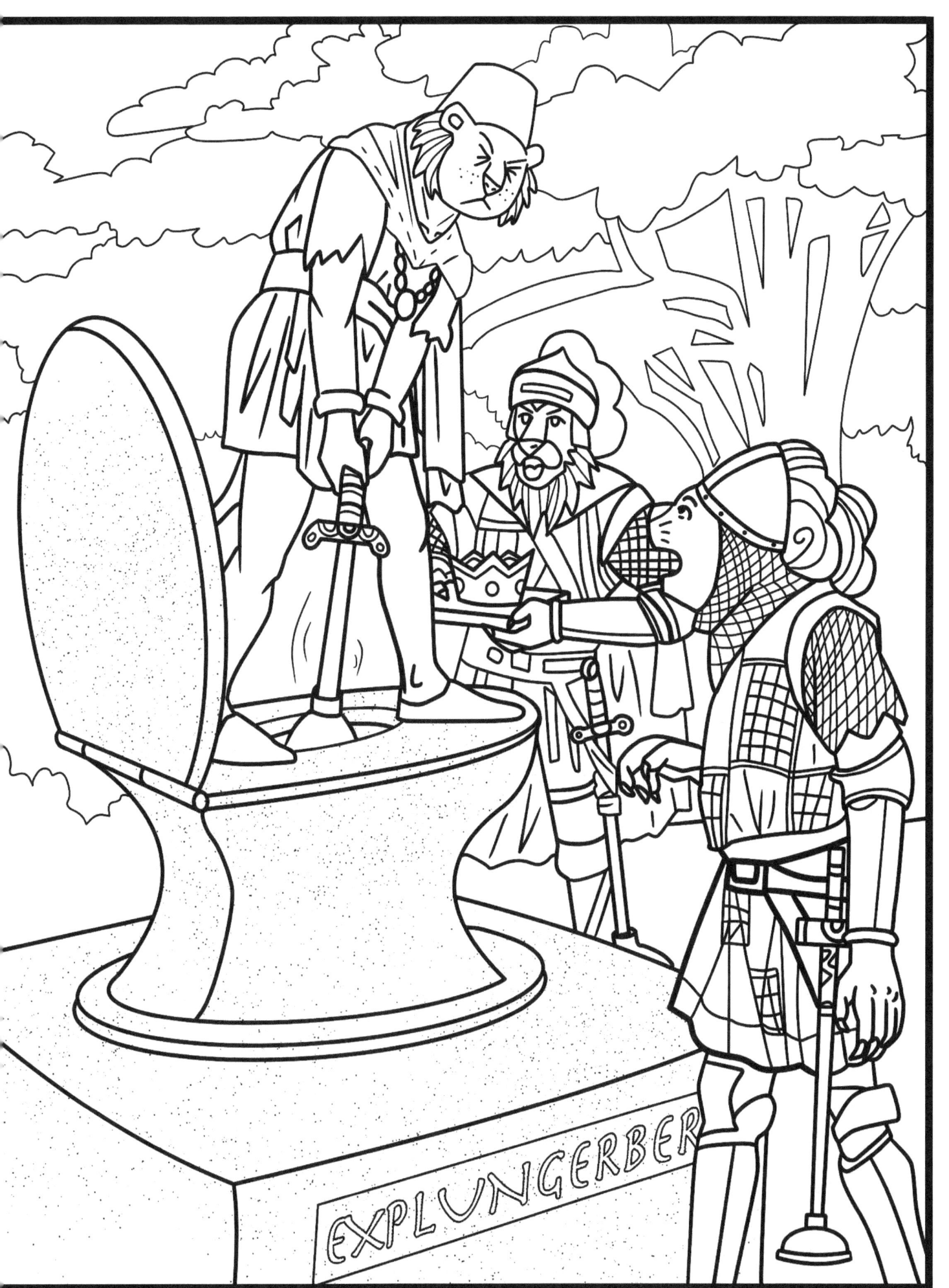

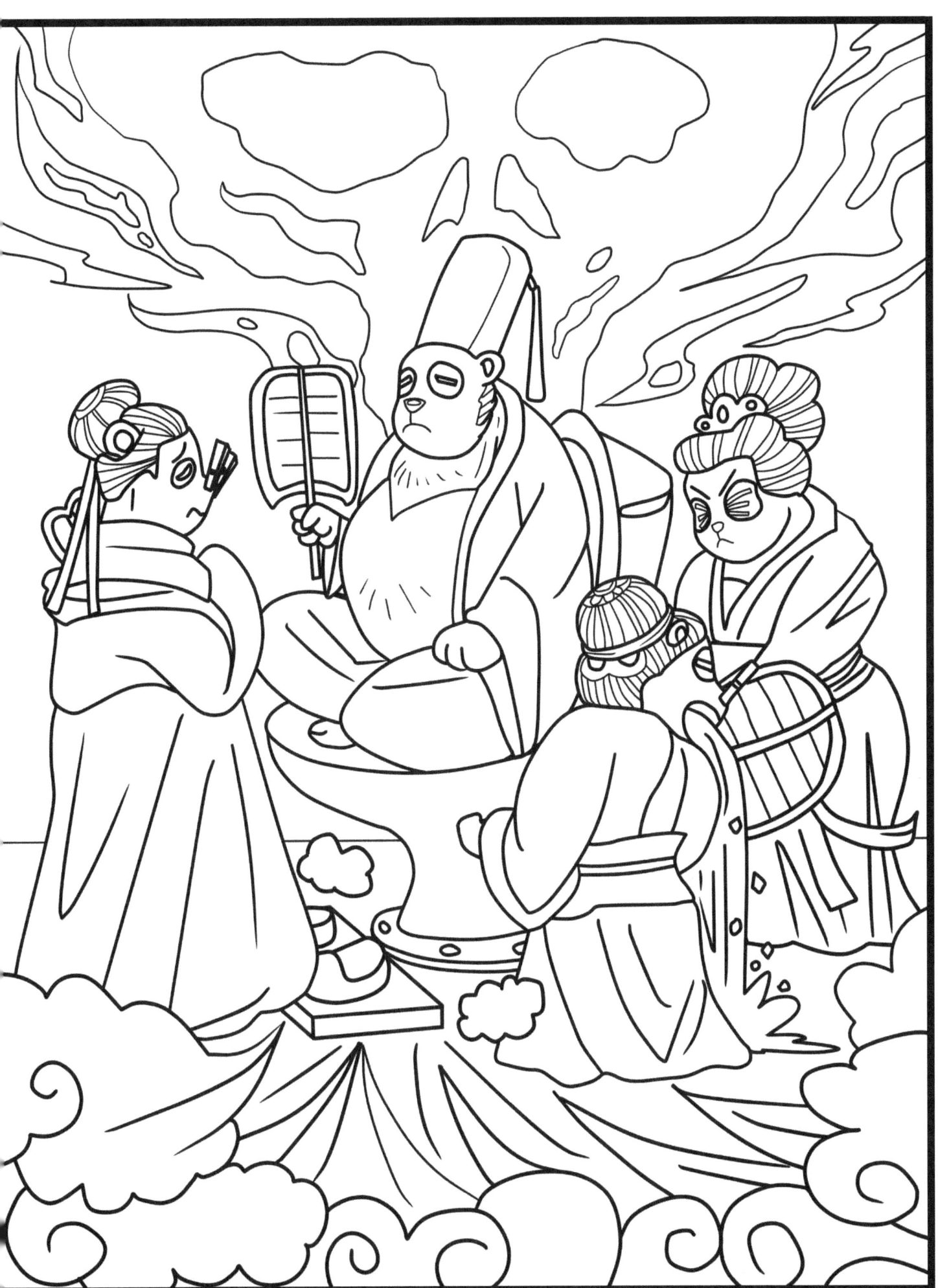

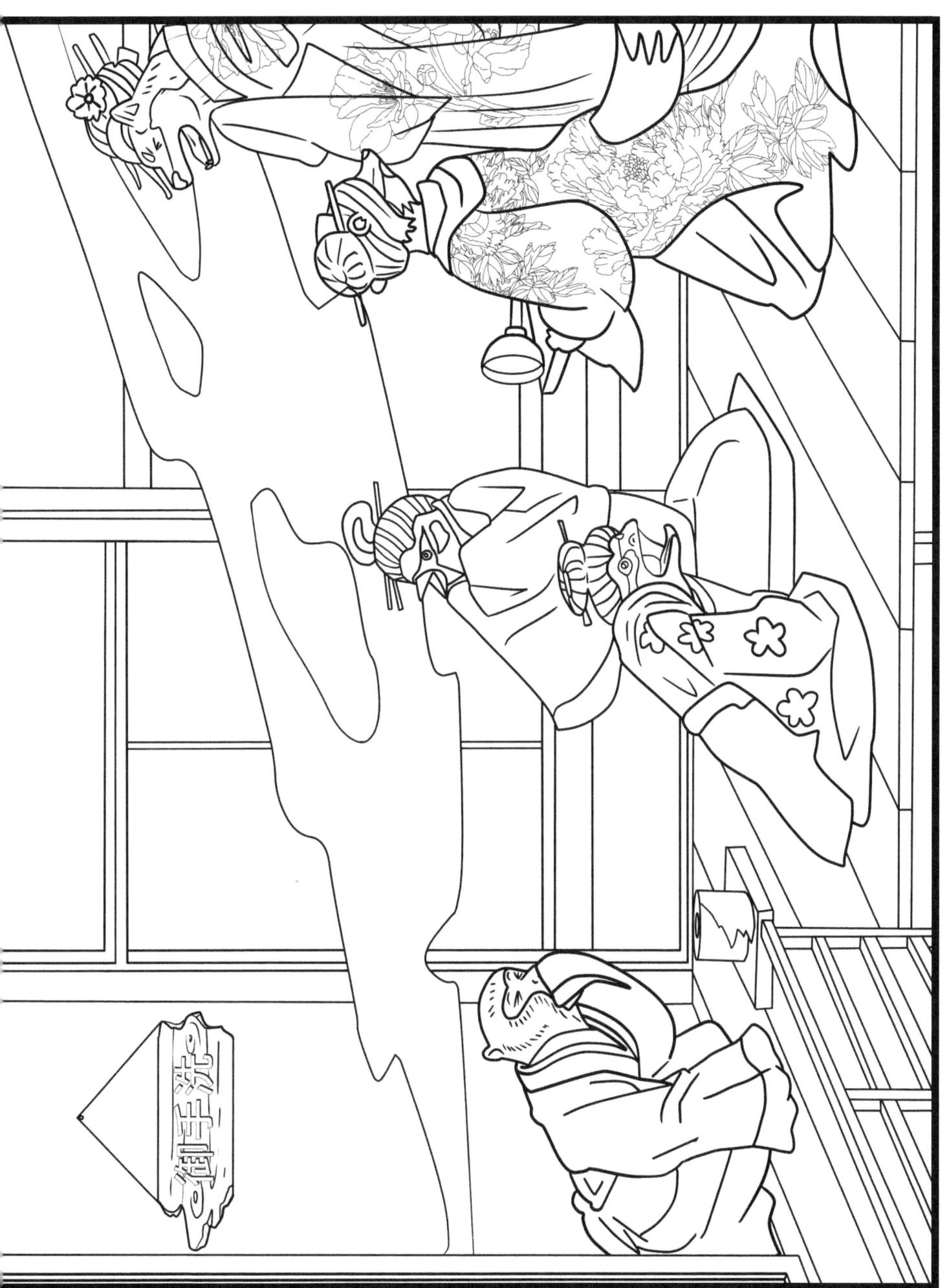

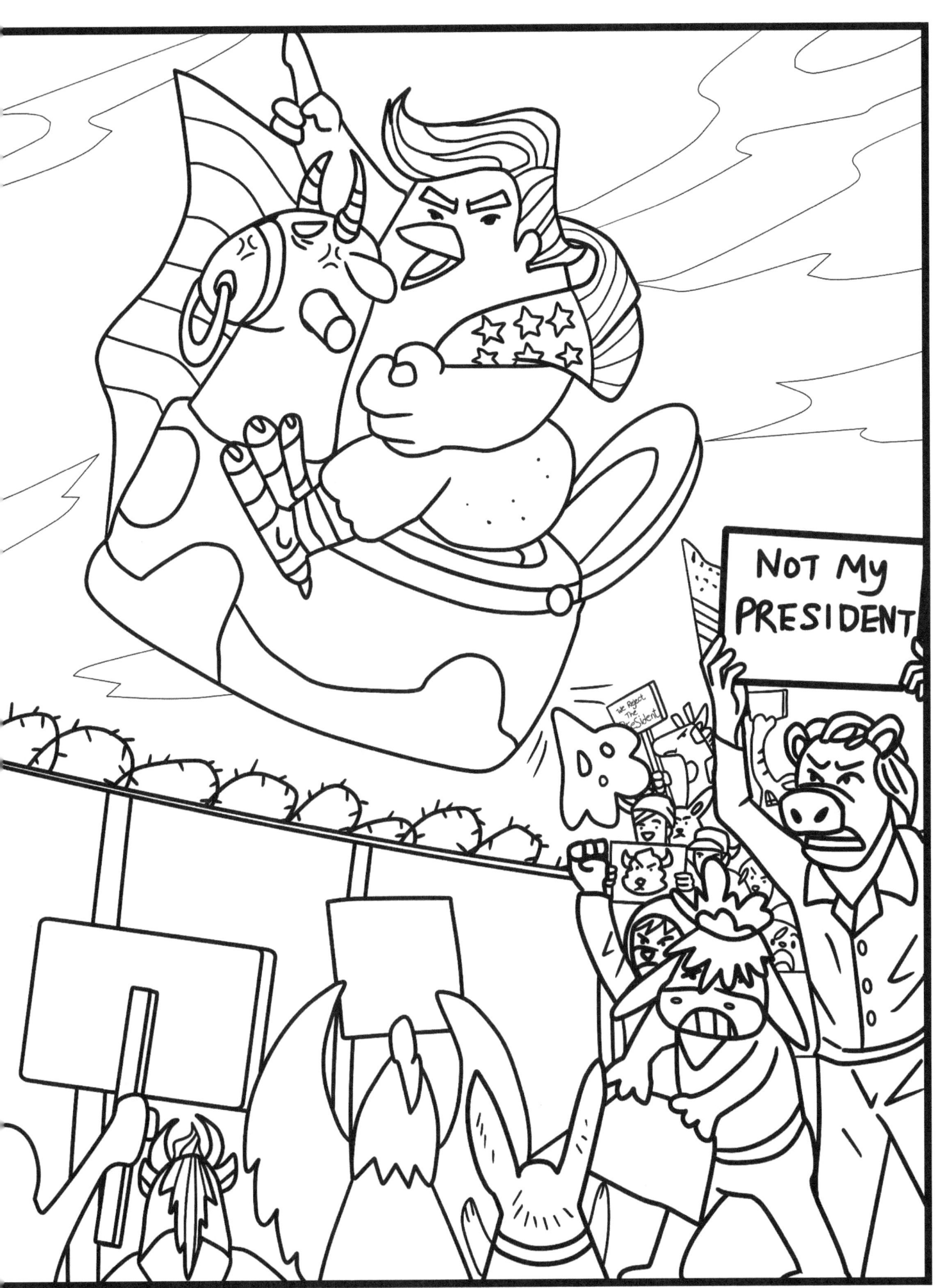

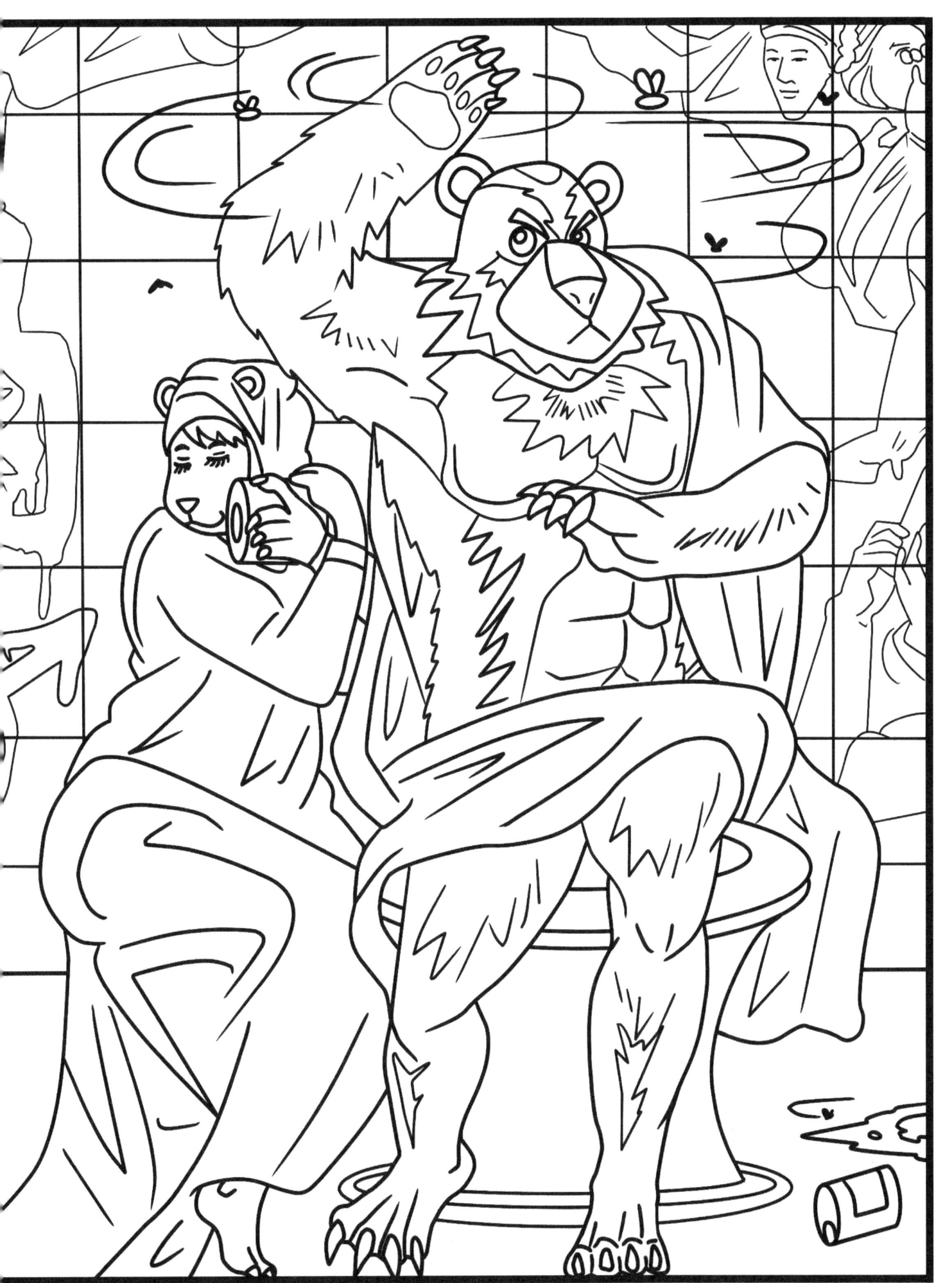

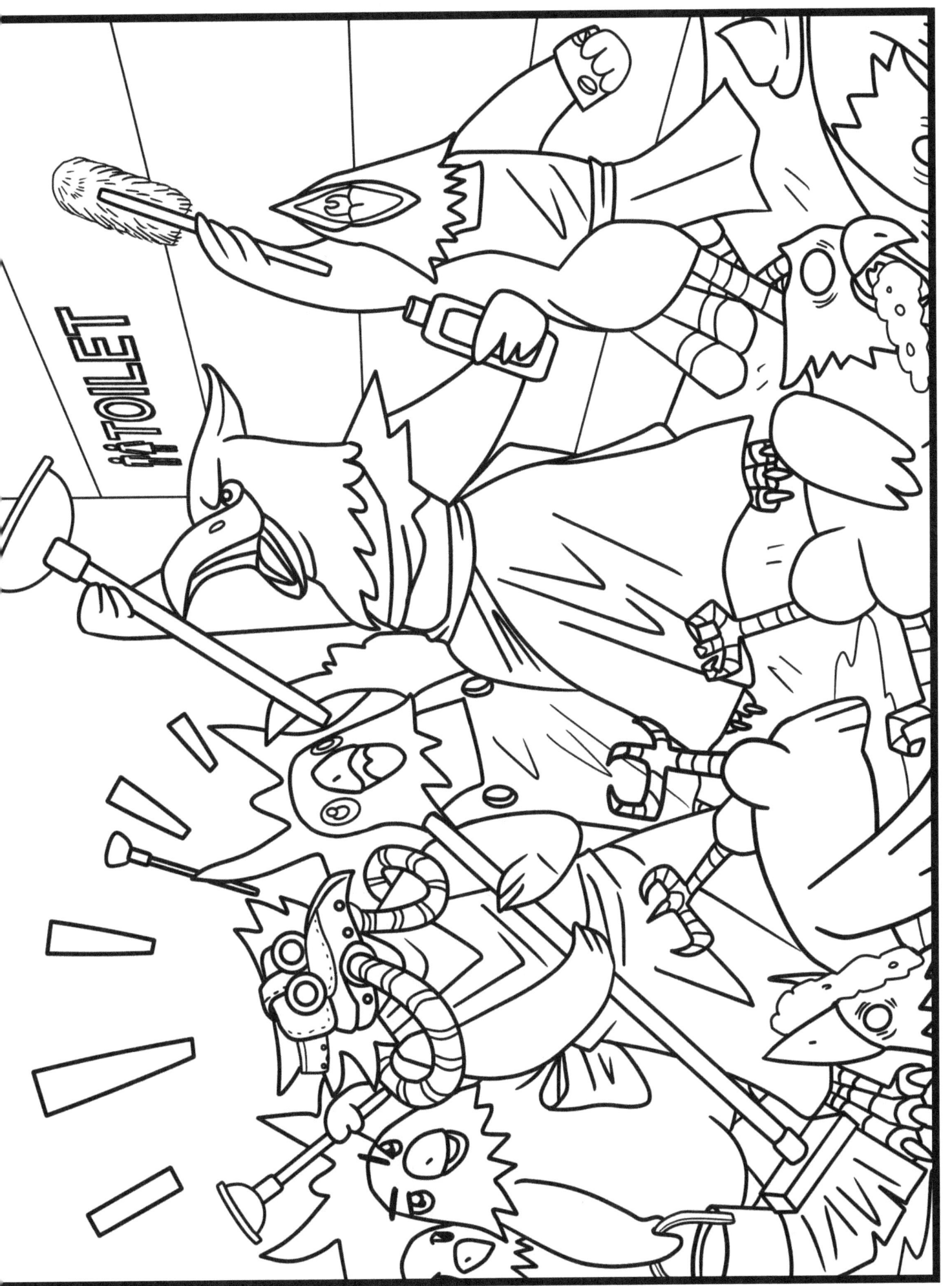

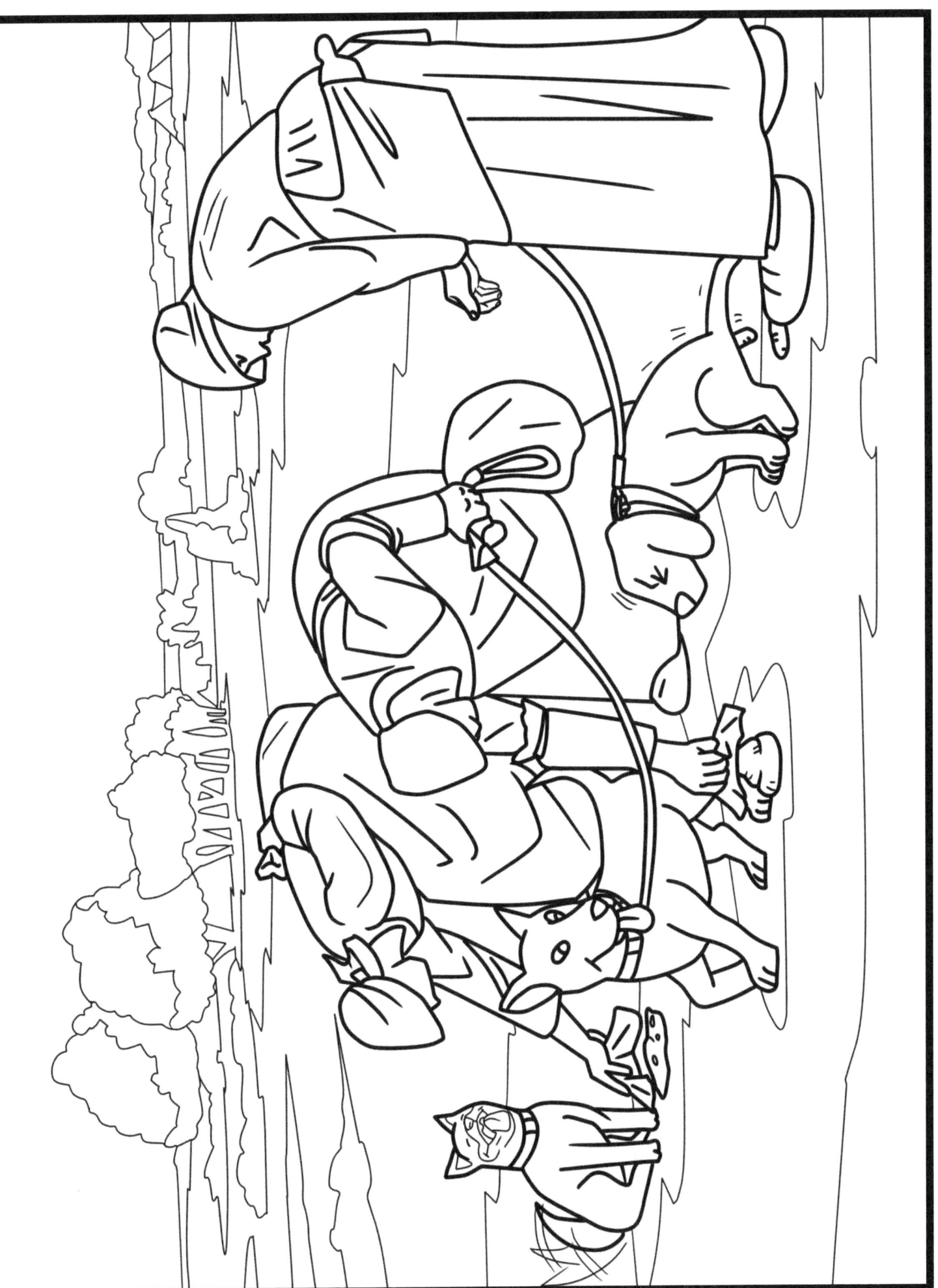

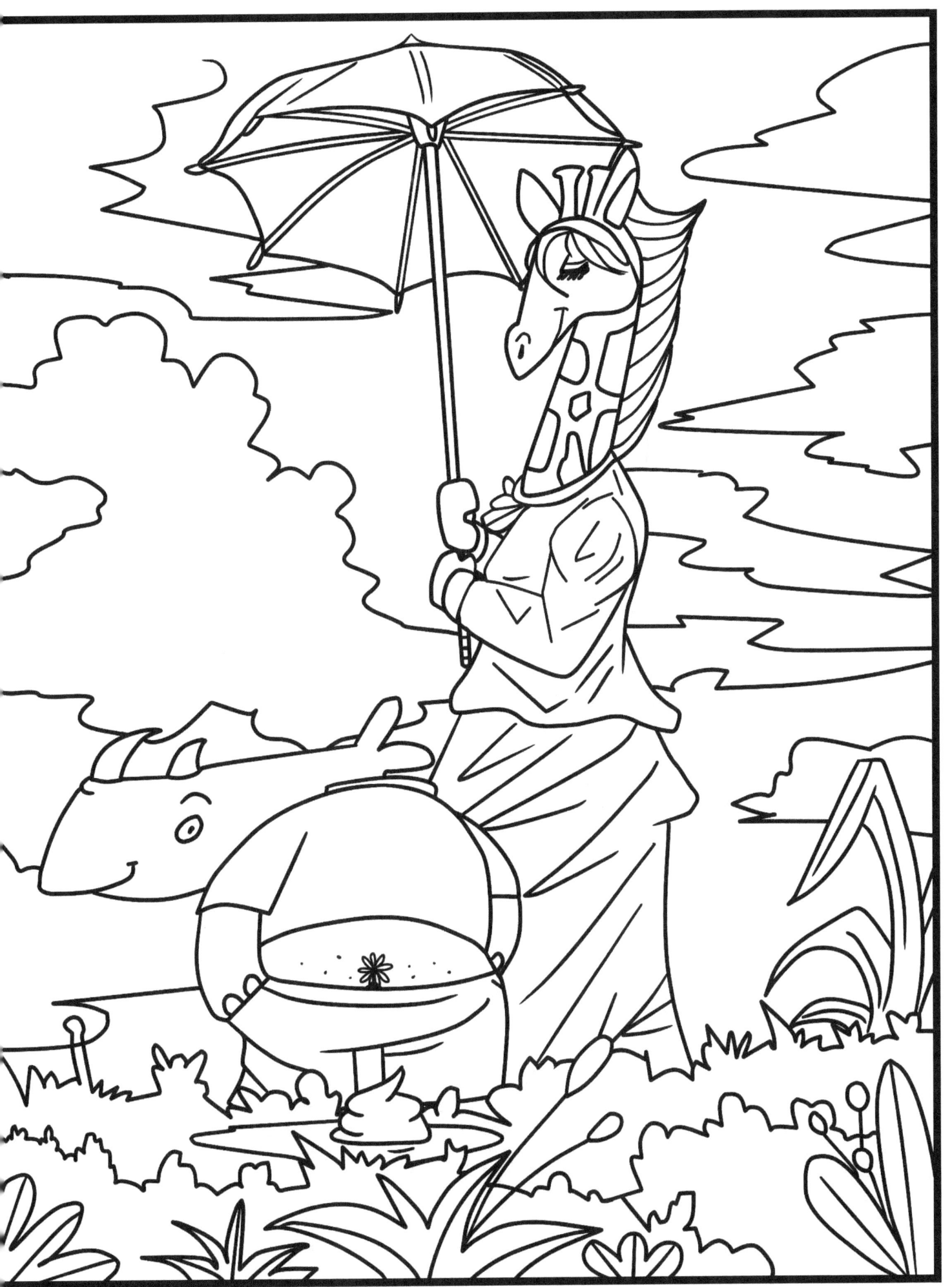

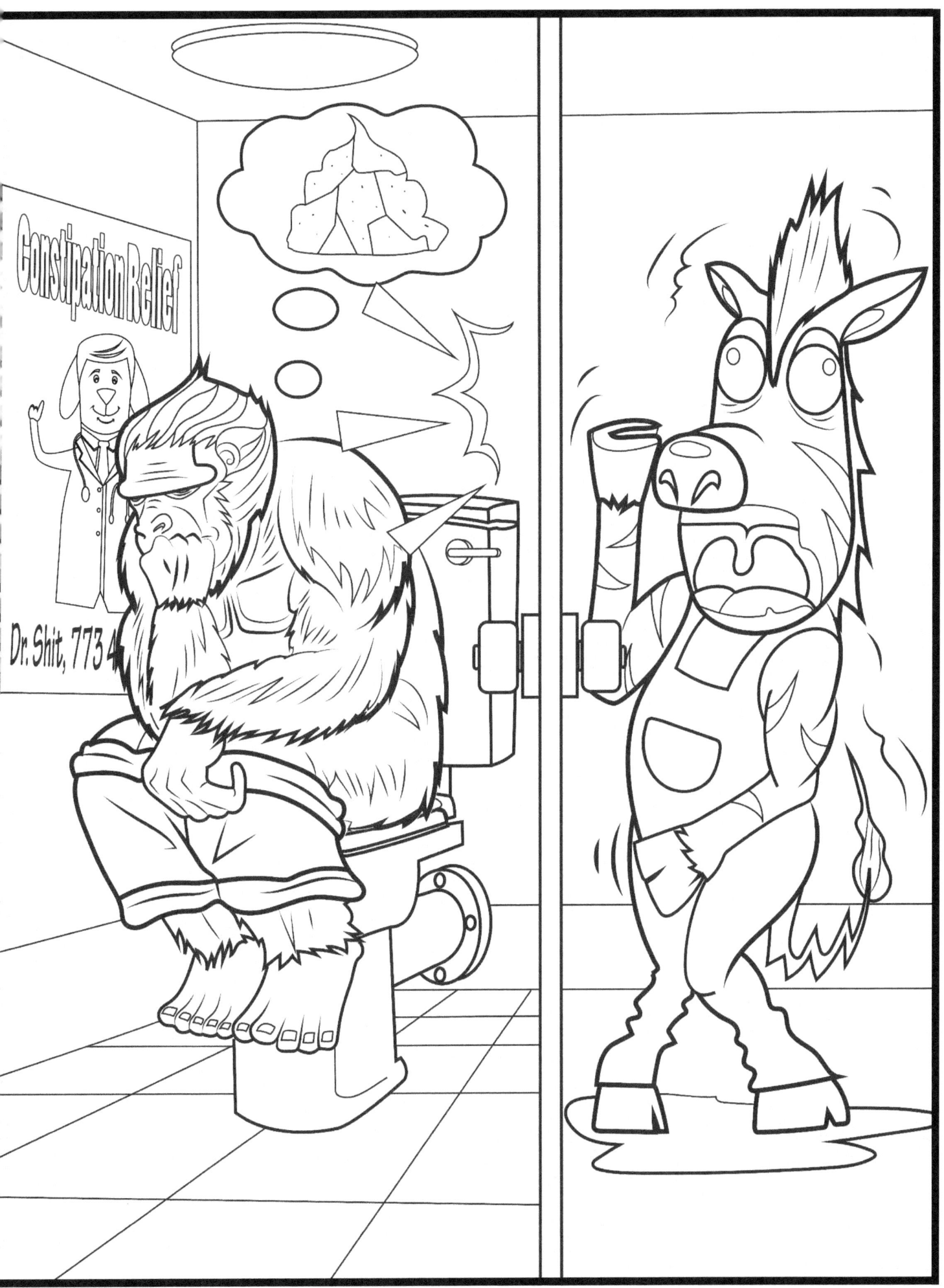

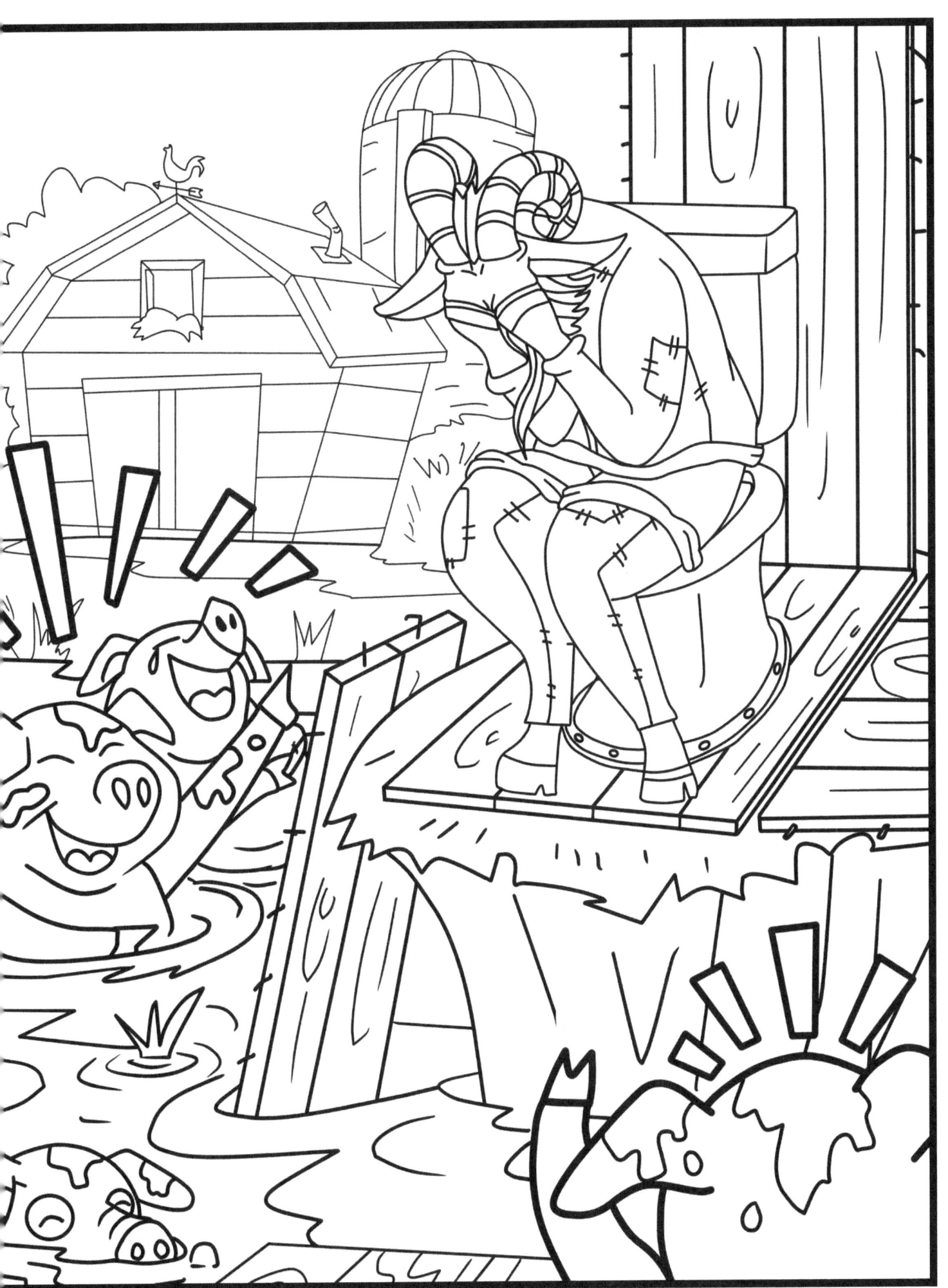

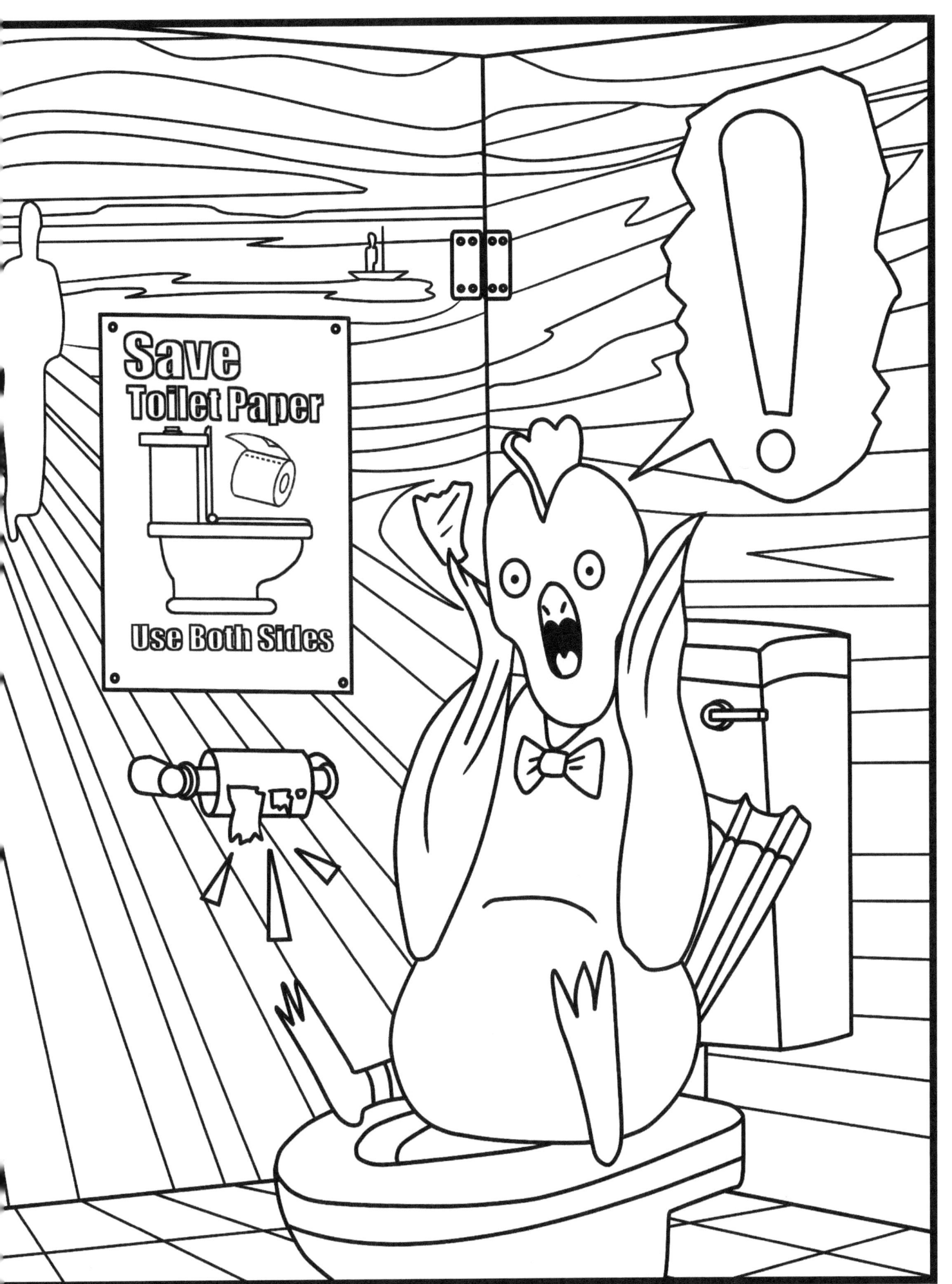

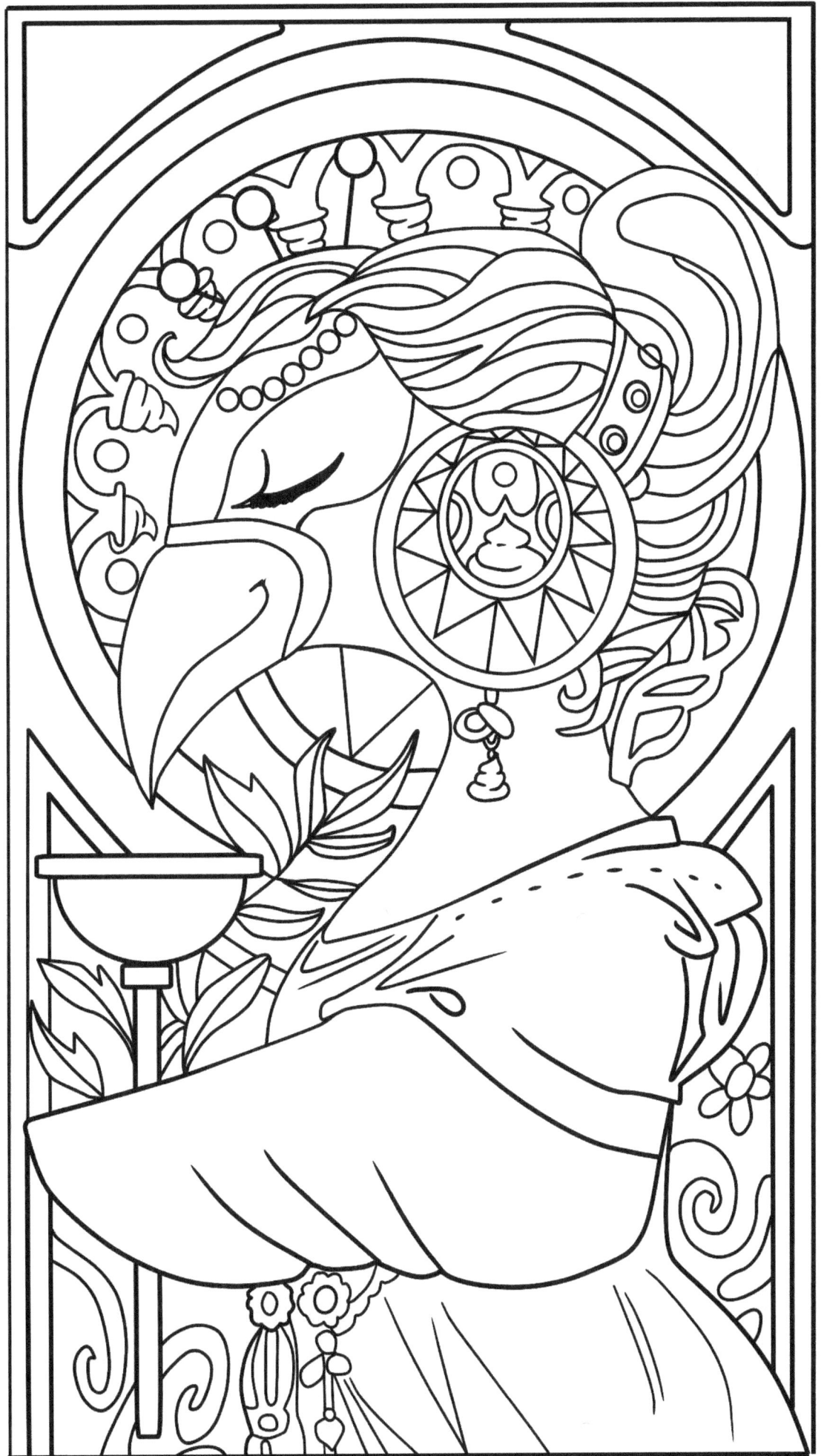

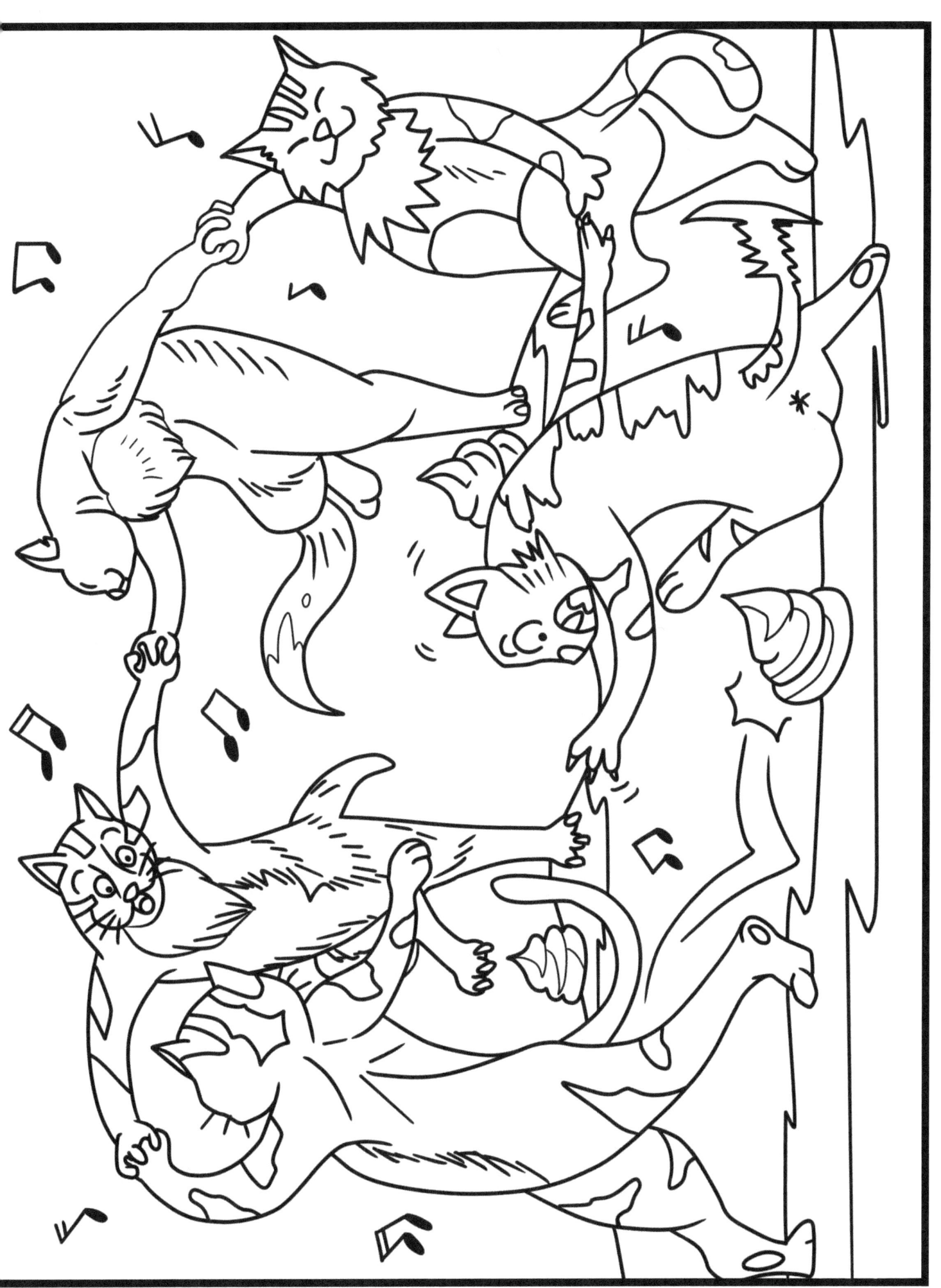

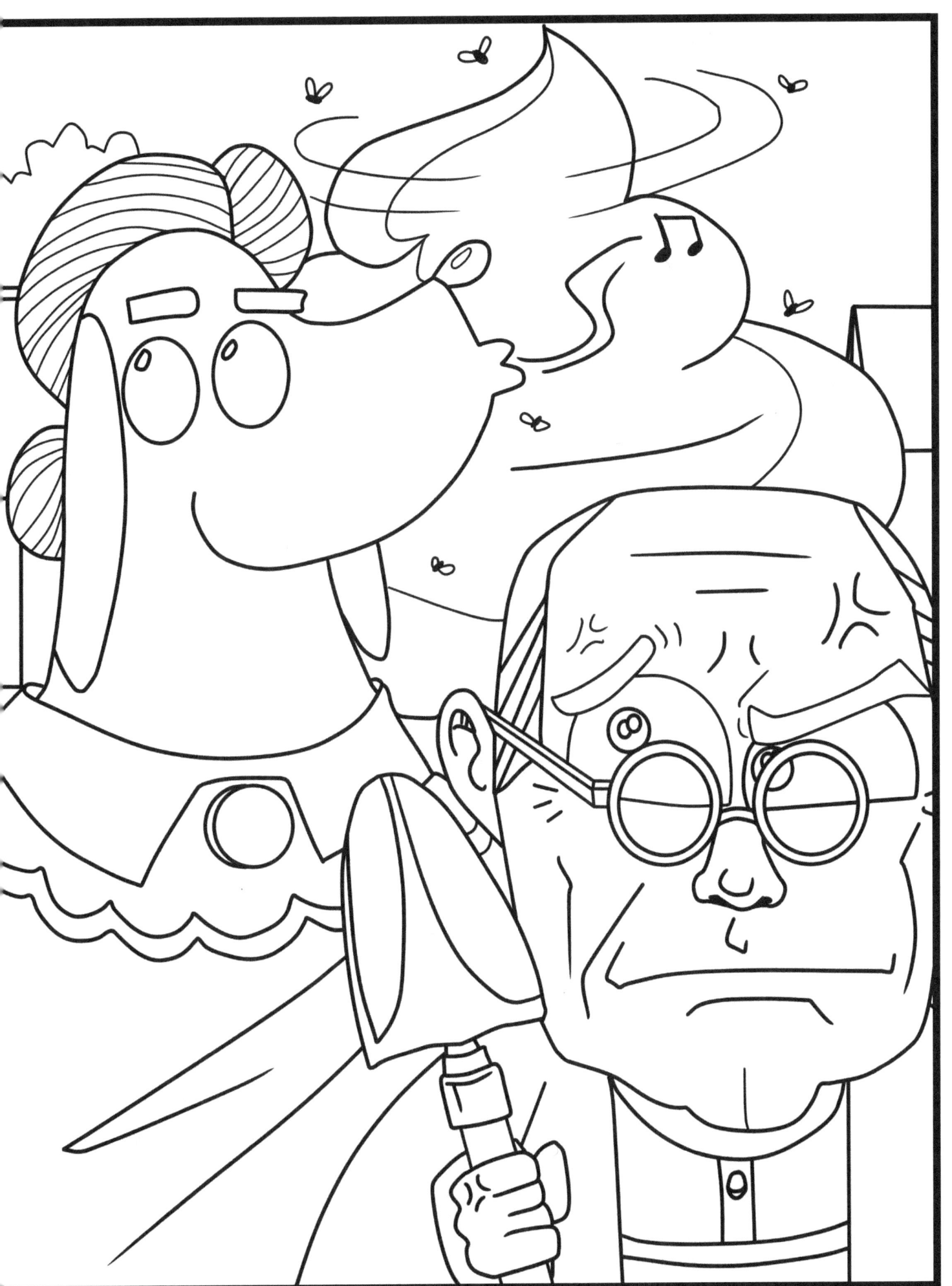

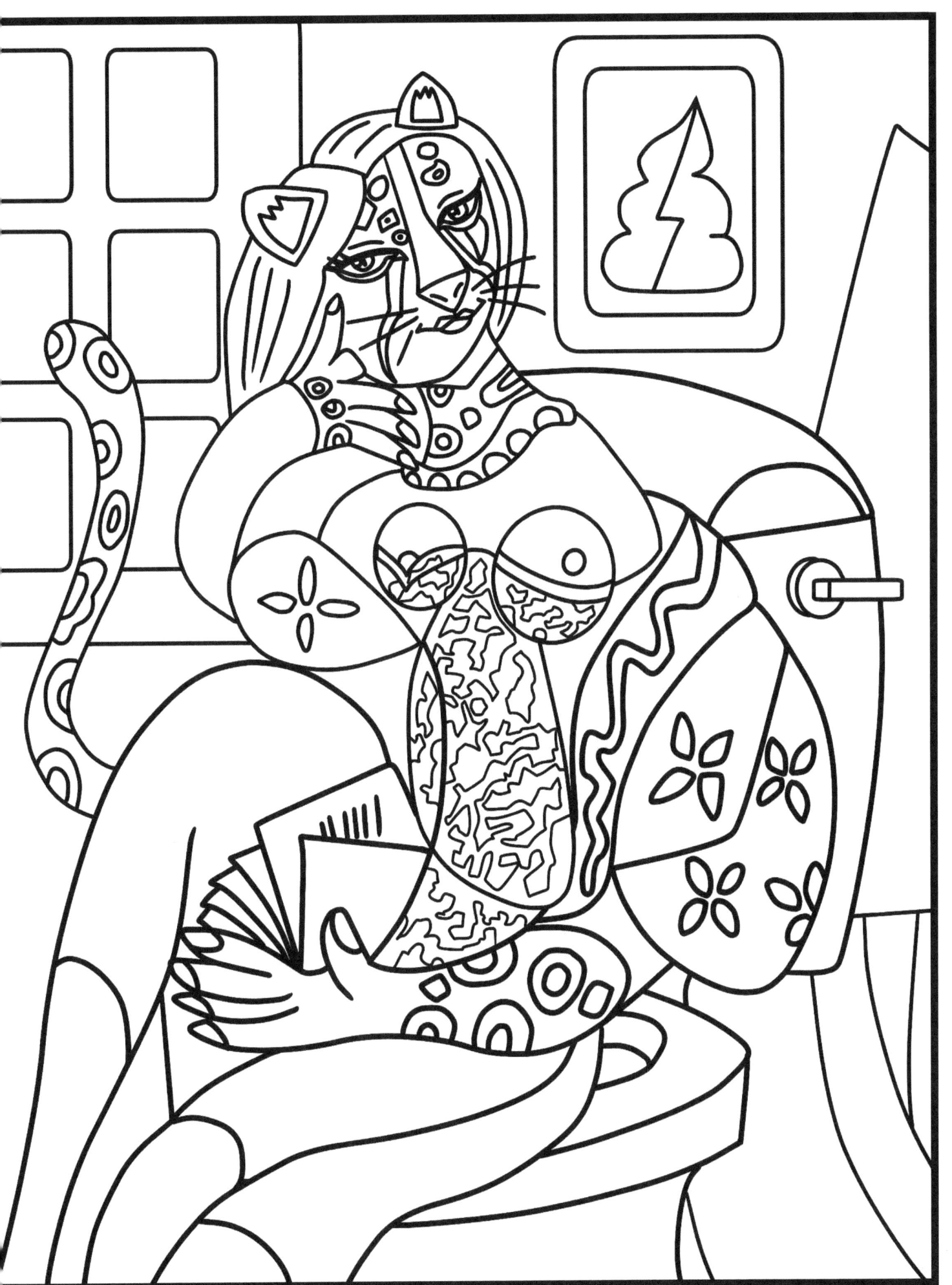

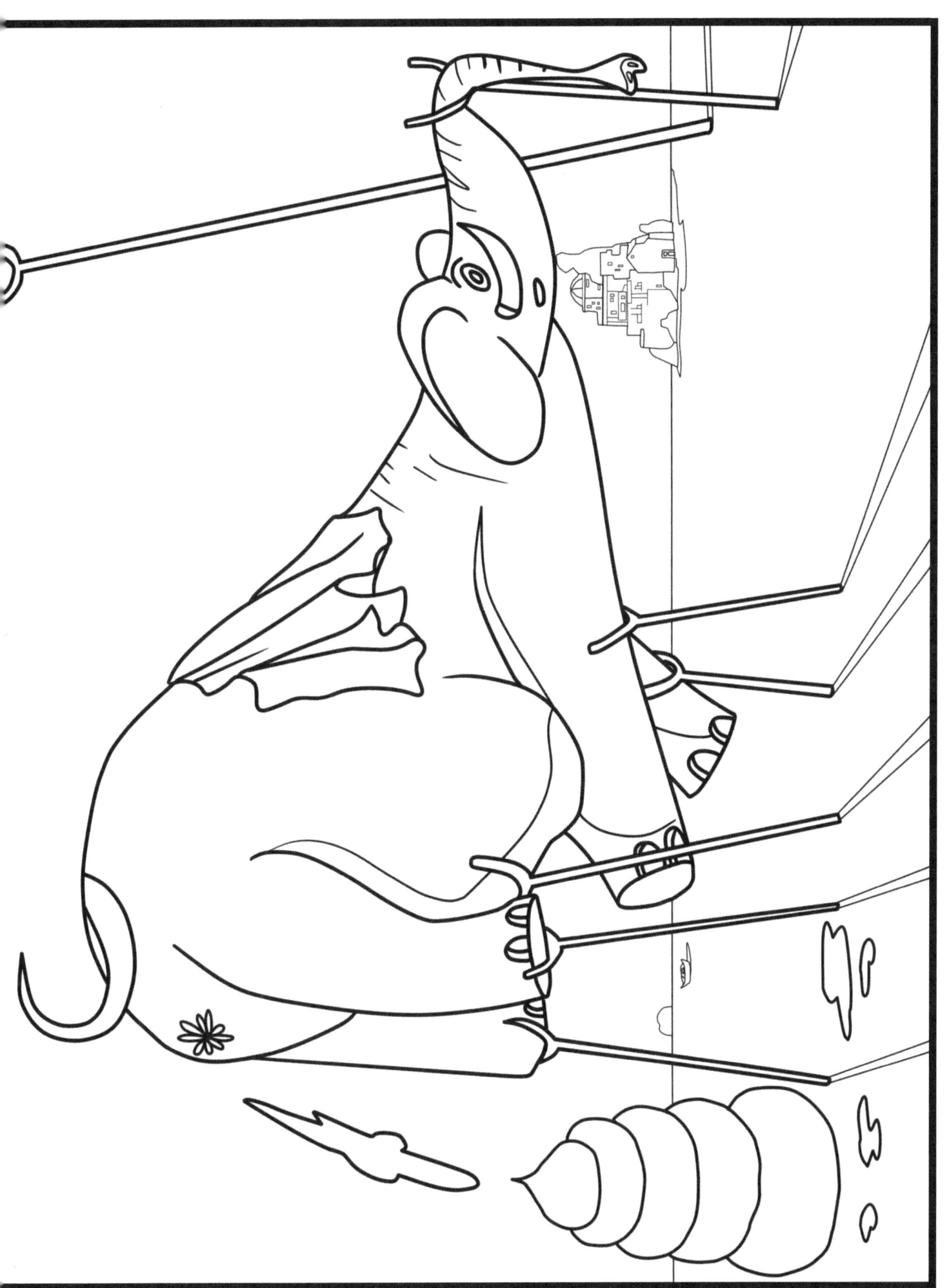

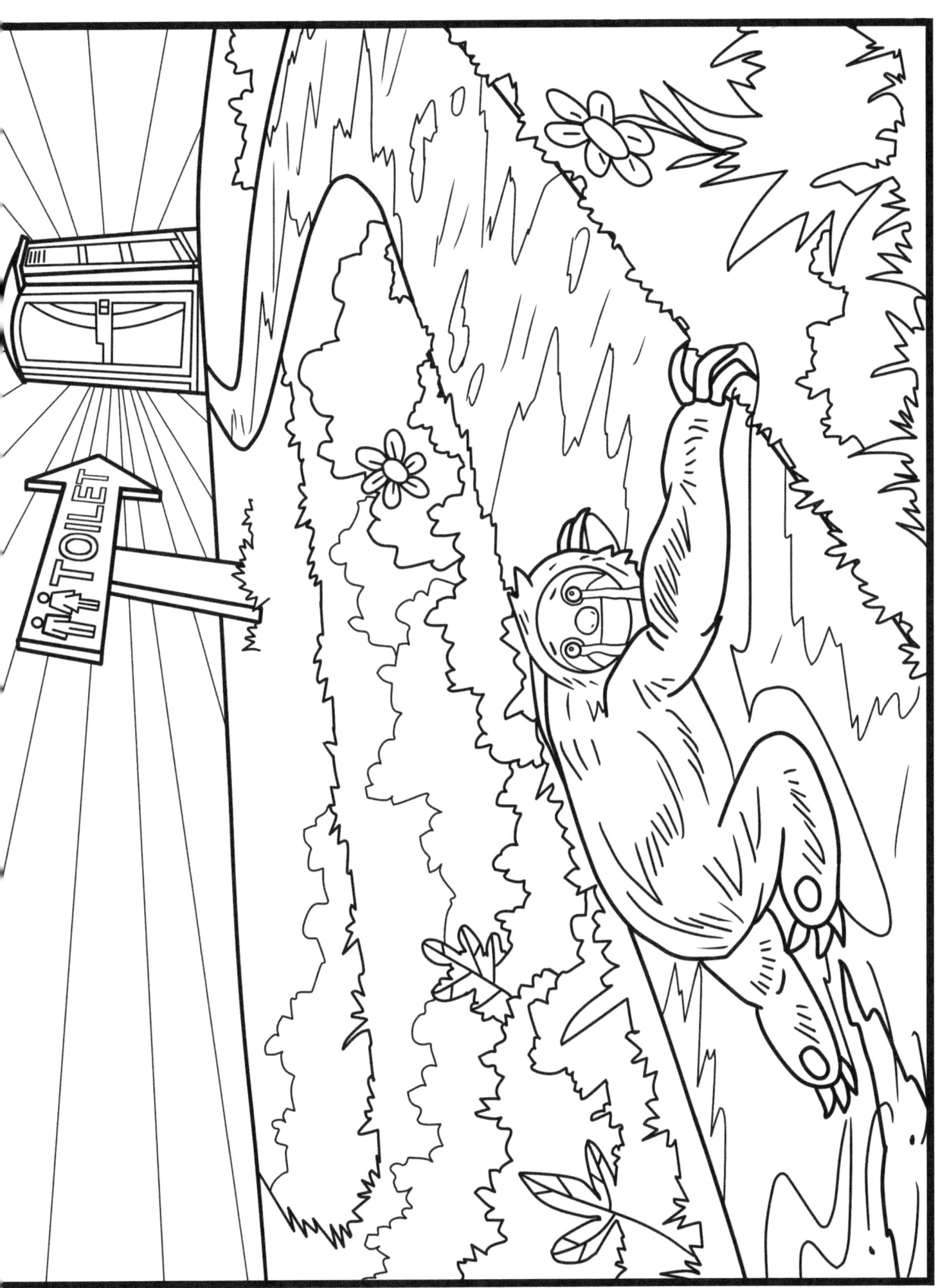

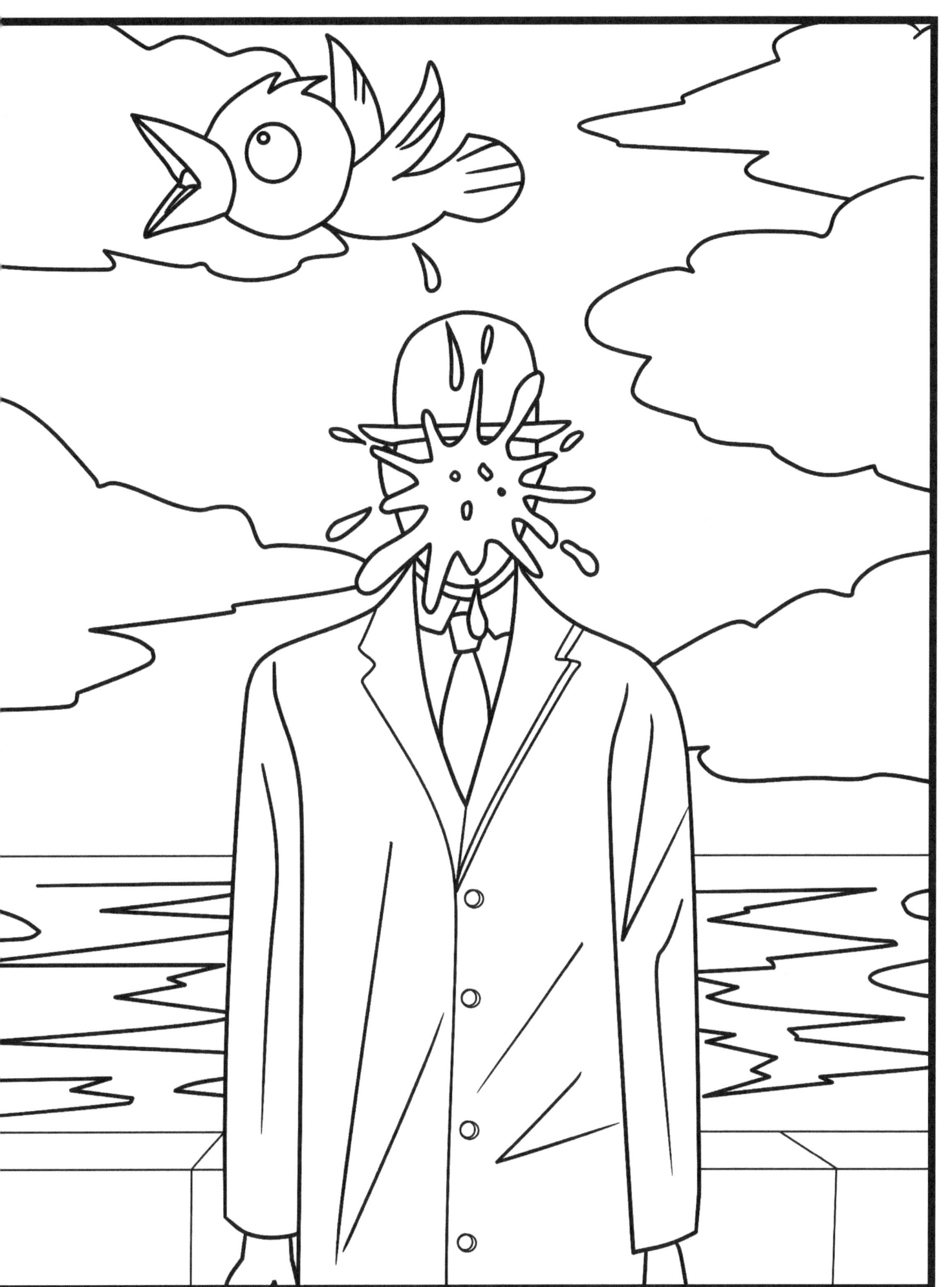

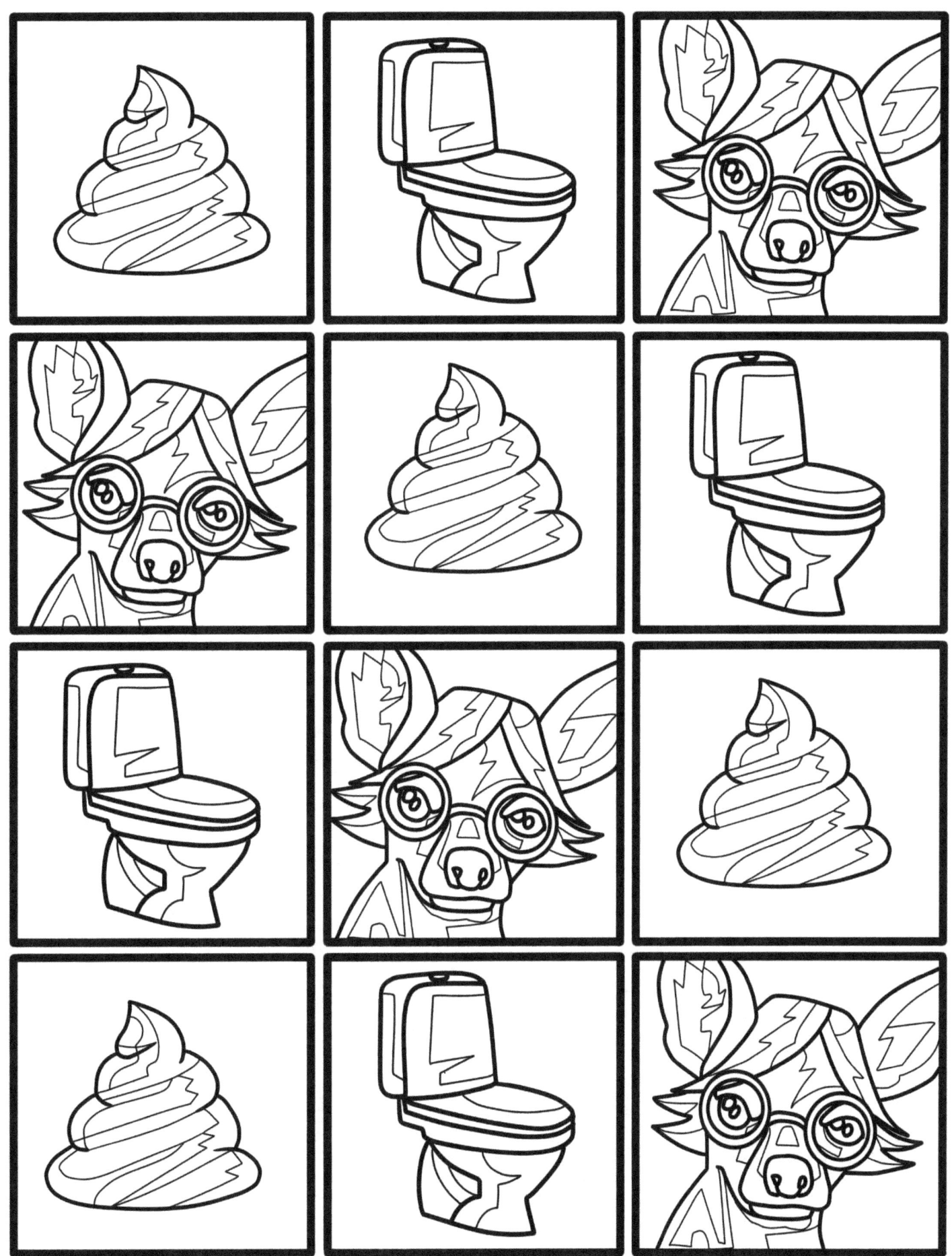

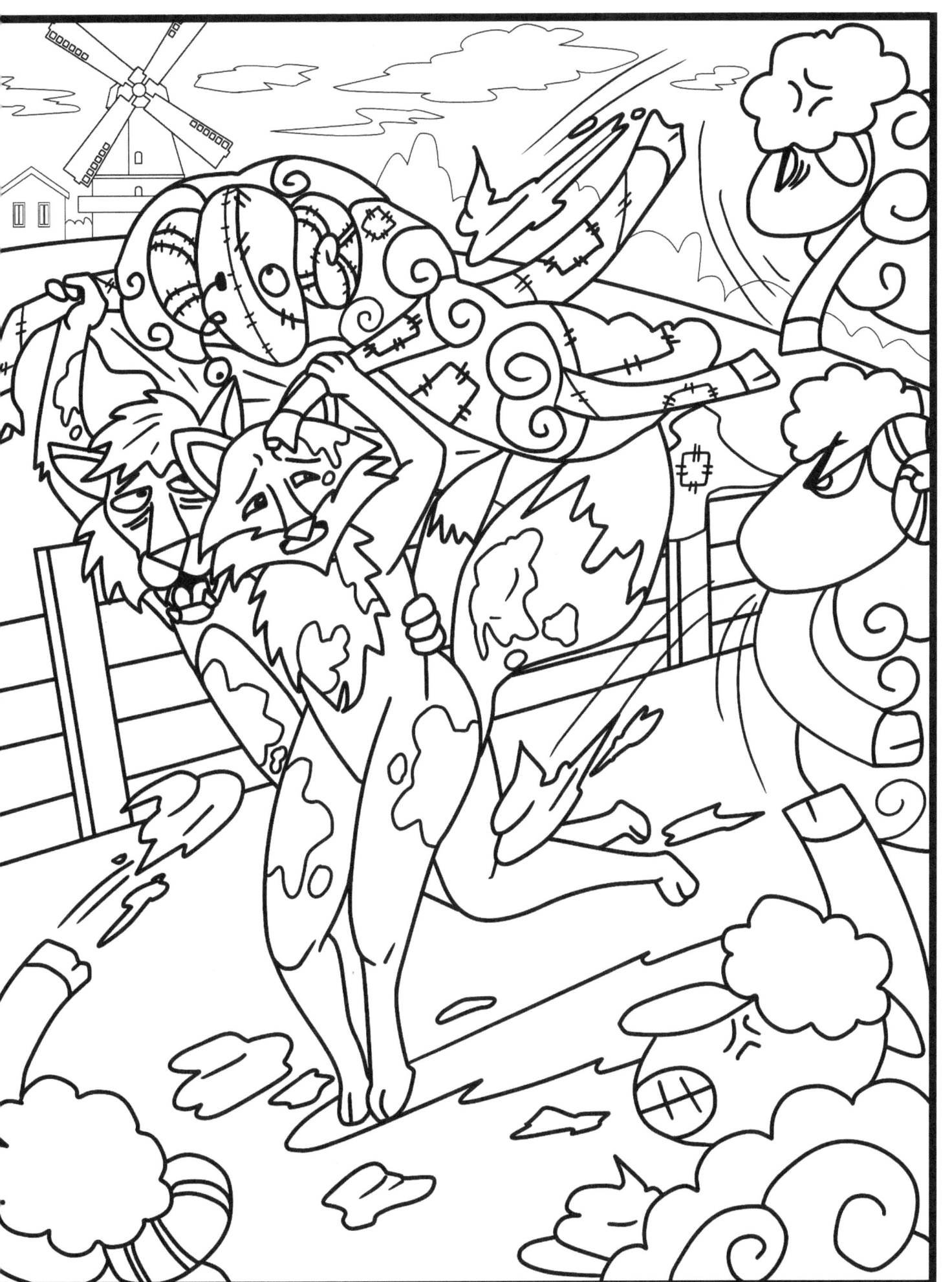

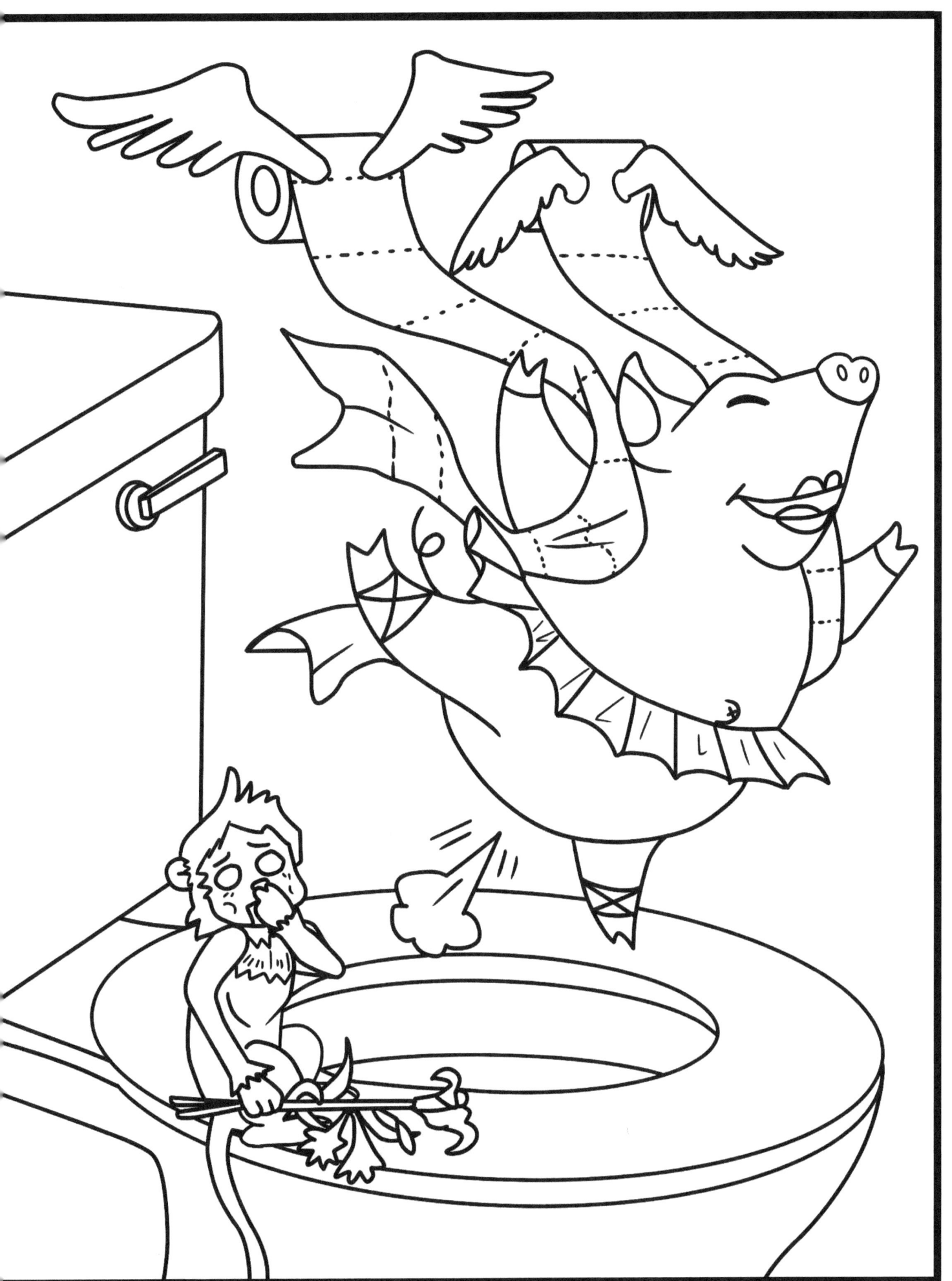

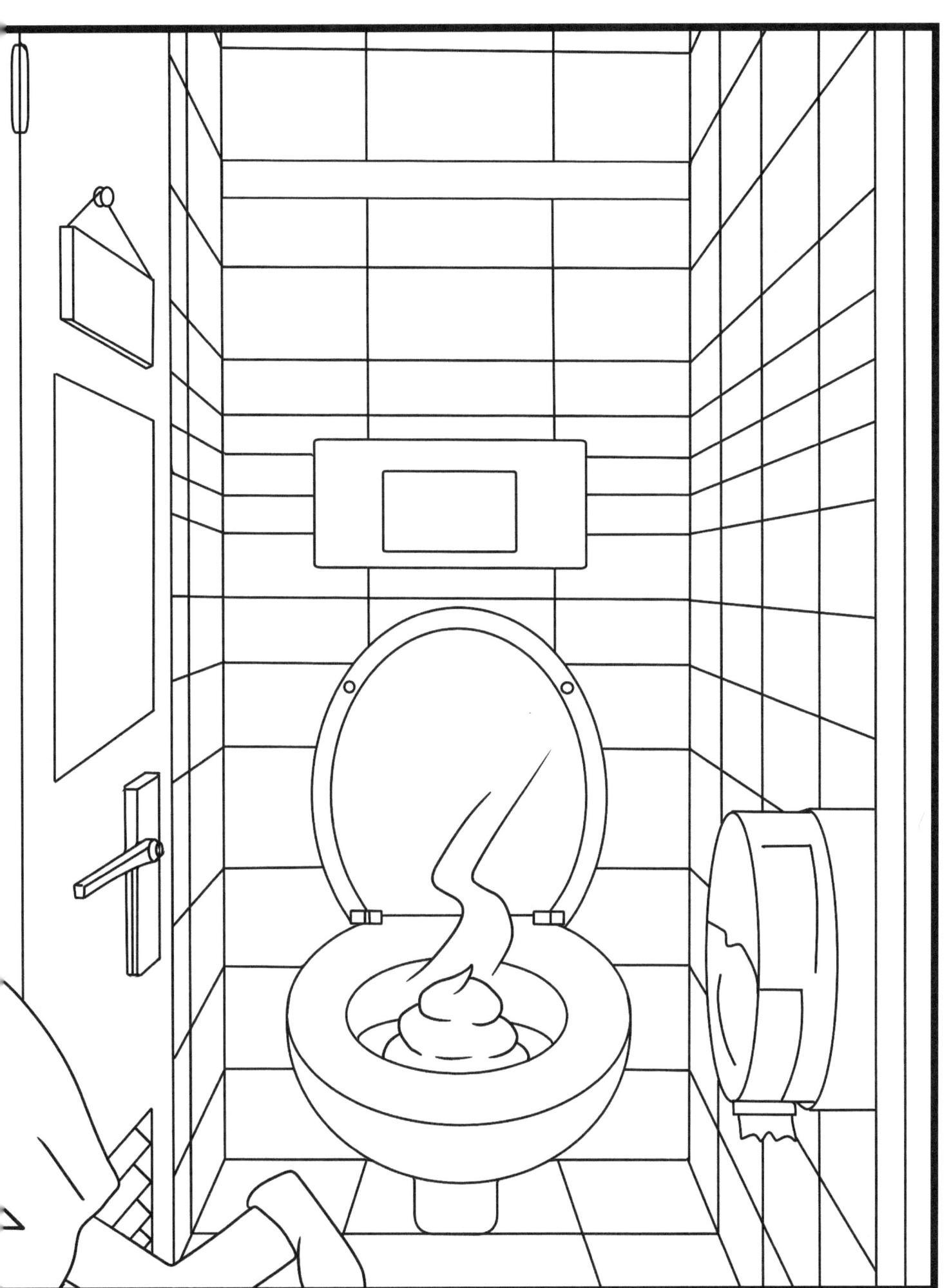

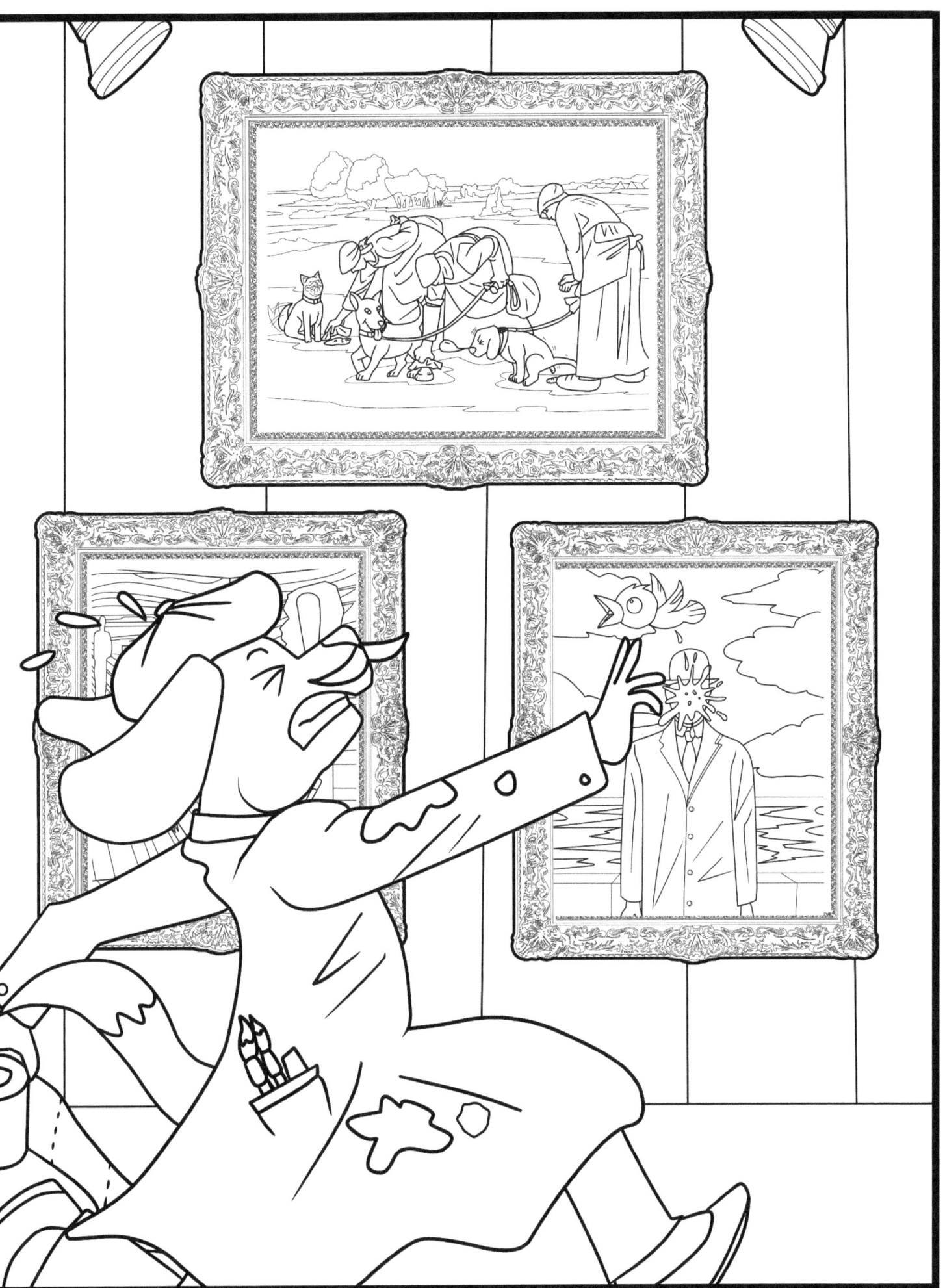

We have now come to an end of our pooptastic journey. How did you like it? Which design was your favorite?

There is a surprise for you on the next page – a greyscale design inspired by Lisa See's famous historical fiction, Snow Flower and the Secret Fan.

Our next cultural journey starts from there. Come along and let's go visit some beautiful girls in East Asia.

To tell us what you think or follow us:

Email: tianyekdp@gmail.com
Facebook: Yao Tian Coloring Books

Please also check our first coloring book: Gateway to China, which is available on both Amazon and Etsy.

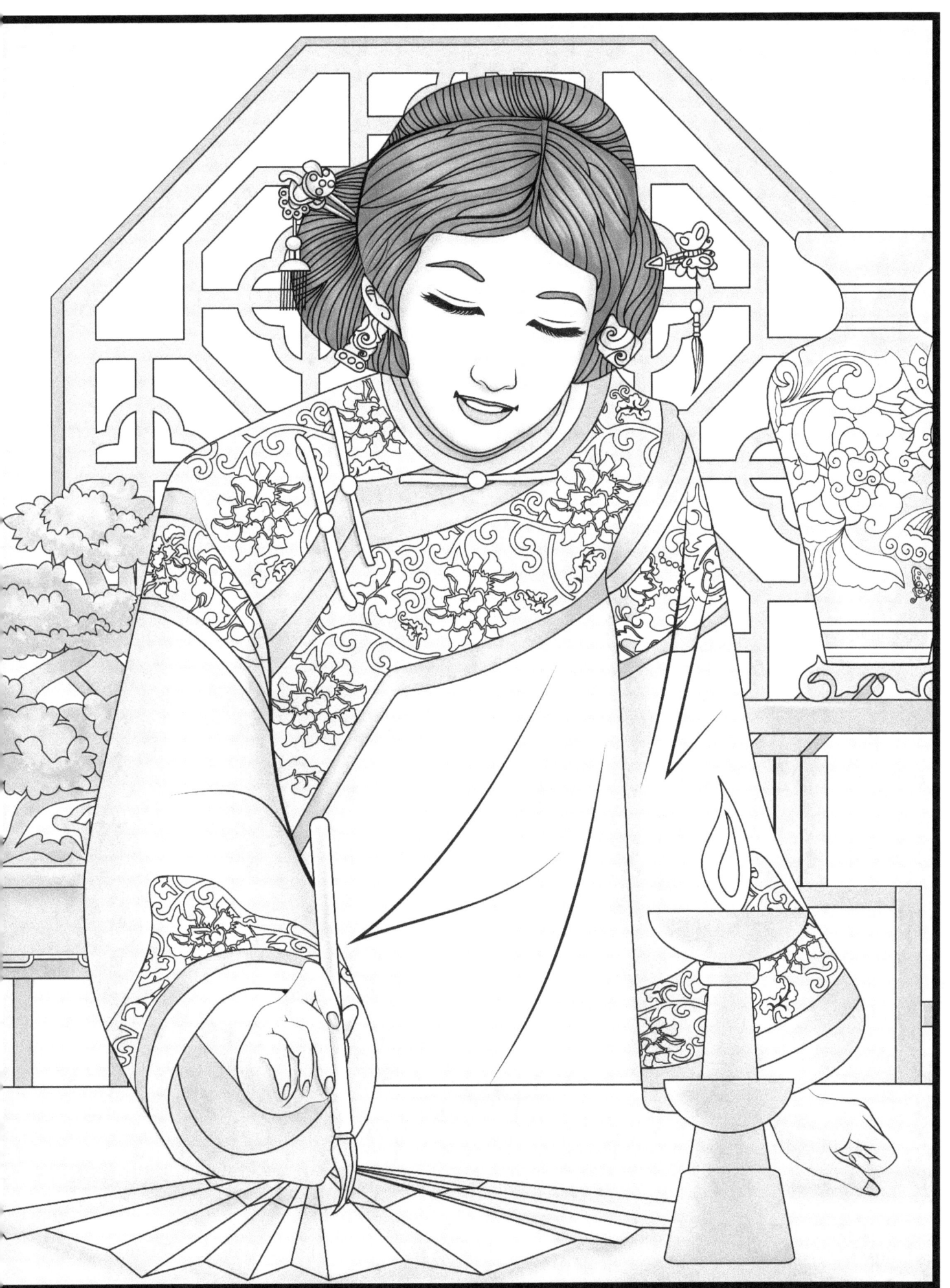

www.ingramcontent.com/pod-product-compliance
Lightning Source LLC
Chambersburg PA
CBHW060002230526
45472CB00008B/1914